Contents

35 Home-Based Business Startups for Under $500

Work from Home, Be Your Own Boss, Make Money Your Way

Find Your Passion!

By

Susan Baker

Published by:

CSBA Publishing House

Cover & Interior designed

By

Rebecca Jackson

First Edition

Prologue: My Story and Special Thanks

First of all, please indulge me in sending a shout-out to a few important people. I would like to thank my parents, who, as small business owners themselves, taught me the value of a dime and hard work. Secondly, I would like to thank my friend Teresa Holmes for letting me bounce ideas off her. Thank you for being the first to read my labor of love!

My story started when I was just 13 years old. I decided

that I absolutely needed tickets to see The Backstreet Boys in concert. Tickets were, of course, terribly expensive and sold out fast. I knew that I needed money. Being a responsible young lady, I decided to start my own neighborhood babysitting service.

I had a name, too, "The Blanchard Street Babysitting Service." I created flyers (probably in MS Paint or something like that at the time) and printed them out at the library. I went to every parent on my block, door to door, handing them a paper and giving my sales speech. I only charged $2/hour per child. At that rate, I would have had to have babysat every child on the block every day for at least two weeks straight to be able to afford those concert tickets.

I wanted to make myself marketable, so I decided to take the American Red Cross Babysitting Certification class. At the end of my Saturday morning training, I had learned about emergency preparedness and some simple first aid – enough to call for help when need be. I made sure to add this qualification to my marketing material.

Pretty soon, I had regular date night gigs with some of my

neighbors who knew my parents. Did I make enough money in time for the concert? No, but I had pocket money for the ice cream truck that came around, and pretty soon, I had saved enough to buy my own new school clothes for the next school year. Thankfully, to reward my initiative, my parents agreed to buy the concert ticket! My mom chaperoned me, and I will never forget the absolute sea of screaming teen girls that I wrapped myself into on the best night of my life.

Seeing the immediate fruits of my labor, my entrepreneurial spirit was born! Ever since, I would consider myself a Business Starter of sorts. I have launched, lost, sold, won, and missed out on several different business opportunities; many are listed in this book.

My latest venture is that of being an author. To support my efforts, would you be so kind as to leave a review online where you purchased this book? Online reviews, good or not-so-good, can give me valuable feedback to apply to my next venture. Thank you in advance, and I hope you enjoy this book.

Home Businesses with Start-up Ideas that Cost Less Than $500: Introduction

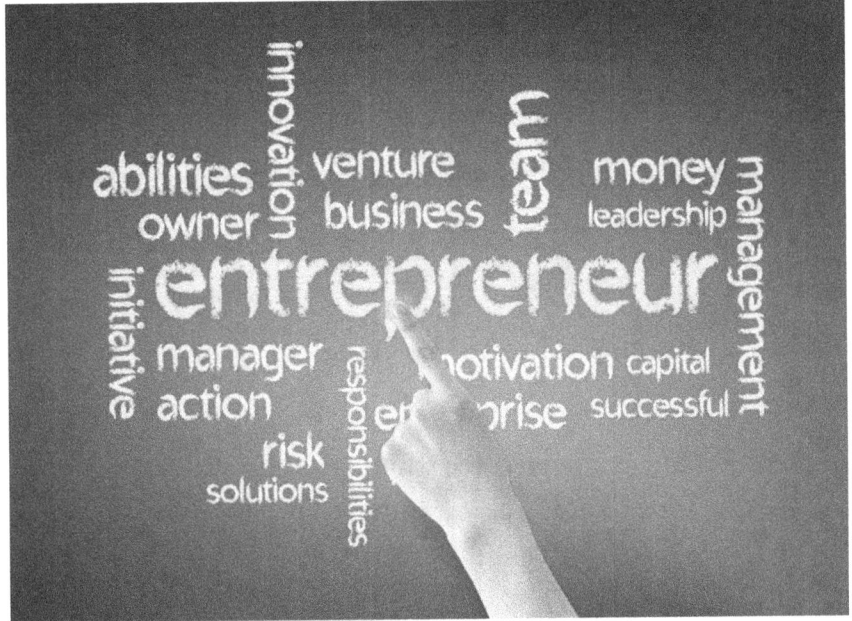

It's easier than ever to build a lucrative career from the comfort of home. If the idea of being your own boss seems like a pipe dream, think again. In the U.S. alone, more than eight million people work from home full-time, some as employees and others as the proprietors of their own businesses.

There are many reasons people choose to work from home, but for the most part, it is the technology that makes them able to do it. Modern technology is opening up the possibility of working from home to an increasing number of people.

Technology is also, at least partially, the reason why so many home-based businesses are succeeding. Today you can fix a bug on a network server on the other side of town or join a meeting half-way across the world without leaving your sofa; work product can be submitted via the internet; documents can be downloaded, signed, and scanned electronically; and phone calls can be re-routed and connected to various locations in a manner of seconds.

But it's not just the work technology enables us to do that is helping so many home-based businesses succeed; it's also the work technology prevents us from doing. Americans, in particular, seem to be busier than ever.

Technology has helped us work faster, but it's also the

reason we're working longer. Not only are we "always connected," but international operations and business dealings are commonplace today, which means more and more people are working odder and/or longer hours.

And that, coupled with the fact that the majority of American families rely on two incomes to survive, has led to an increase in the number of successful home-based, service-related small businesses.

When it comes down to it, people don't always have the time (or energy) to do the things they need to do (or would want to do) if there were only enough hours in the day. Small businesses that fulfill basic domestic needs are on the rise. And it doesn't take a specialized skill, college education, or loads of up-front financing to start one.

Working from home isn't always easy and starting a new business does require sacrifice (more on both those points in the next chapter), but If you have the drive, the will-power and the desire to do it, chances are you have what it takes to be your own boss.

This book takes a look at the various types of home-based,

low-cost start-ups that are finding success in the modern marketplace.

Chapter One: Risky Business

Owning a home-based business and being your own boss may be the dream, but that doesn't mean it's one that comes without sacrifice. It takes hard work and dedication to run a business and, even more so, to start one.

Before we get into the basics of starting a business from home, we first must consider the risks of starting a home-based business. Keep in mind, the negatives aren't meant to discourage you. Rather, they are included here to prepare you for the road ahead.

There's always some risk when starting a business, even one with low start-up costs, and it's important to know what they are and when to call it quits. It doesn't matter how good you are at planning; you can't predict the future, and when it comes to starting a business, that's part of the risk.

There's no way to know if a customer will pay late (or not at all), if a delay in shipping will leave you without the equipment/supplies needed to provide your product/service to clients or if the cost of supplies will skyrocket, eliminating your profit on open orders.

The time it takes to turn a profit, and the amount of profit you'll actually earn are two of the biggest risks when starting a business. But they aren't the only one

Before you start your home-based business, consider the following risks and how to mitigate them.

Business Risks:

Liability/Lawsuits

Injury/Illness

Interruptions

Strained Relationships

Security/Data Breaches

Insufficient Funds

Business Failure

Personal Financial Loss

Lawsuits/Liabilities

As a business owner, you'll be exposed to some liability issues. There are two tried and true ways to protect yourself from lawsuits and liability: forming an LLC and getting business insurance. Neither are cheap, and many new business owners opt to wait until money starts coming in before taking on these expenses, but it's imperative that you don't wait too long.

LLCs are hybrid organizations combining the simplicity of a sole proprietorship with the protection of incorporation. They lack the burdensome requirements of incorporation and protect owners from personal liability.

In other words, if you get sued, only your business assets are on the line. Your personal vehicle, home, bank accounts, and other assets remain safe. We'll cover them further in the next chapter. The type and amount of insurance needed to reduce liability vary based on the type of business and the nature of your product or service. For example, a home-run catering business has greater liability than a home-run graphic design business because of the risks of foodborne illnesses and injury.

Injury/Illness

If you're generally healthy, you might dismiss the possibility of illness as a risk, but it's worth consideration.

What happens if you become injured or ill and are unable to fulfill customer orders?

Without a back-up plan in place, you risk losing customers, damaging your reputation, and having to use personal funds to cover costs if refunds are needed.

To best protect yourself from these risks, consider contracts that specify specific refund terms and network with like professionals who may be willing to take on the extra workload should you become temporarily out of commission.

If possible, work out a type of mutual aid agreement with a similar business, where you both agree to take on some of the others work at a pre-determined rate, should one of you become temporarily unable to fulfill customer orders.

Interruptions

Not only are you more prone to interruptions from friends and family when working from home, but you also face the risk of temporary and long-term utility interruptions from natural disasters, storms, and fires.

To reduce interruptions from friends and family, consider implementing business hours. And remind people of them as needed.

You can't prevent a natural disaster or power outage, but you can prepare for one. To prevent the loss of customer information and orders, consider using an off-site server or cloud-based back-up system that will allow you to access customer files even if you are unable to access your home office.

It also helps to have a disaster recovery plan in place that identifies how, when, and where you will resume business operations following an interruption.

These types of plans come in handy for both major and minor emergencies. They provide a step-by-step course of action in the aftermath of major disasters and can help you plan ahead when facing minor service interruptions.

Strained Relationships

Starting a business, even one based out of your home requires a lot of time. If you want your business to succeed, you'll need to put in long days. And all those long days can take a toll on your personal relationships.

Good communication can help minimize this strain. Take time to explain the situation to loved ones, then make a point to set aside a little time each night or each weekend to devote to personal relationships.

Depending on the nature of your new business, the business itself may also put a strain on your relationships. This is especially common in sales. Constantly hitting up your friends and family to purchase your Tupperware, skin care products or leggings, brews annoyance and resentment.

Staying organized and developing a level of self-awareness can help in this area.

Keep track of when and how often you make sales pitches to personal acquaintances and make a point to personally thank them and all your customers when they do make a purchase.

Security/Data Breaches

If your business requires the collection of people's personal information or credit cards, it's your responsibility to keep that information safe.

The stolen information, especially credit card information, can result in loss of customers, a ruined reputation, and lawsuits. To protect your customers' information and your business interests, invest time and money in knowing and utilizing an array of security measures.

For hard copy information, consider investing in a locking file cabinet, as well as a home security system.

If you can't afford a home security system, consider using a nanny cam that alerts you to noise and movement when you are away from the office. Dogs are also great deterrents to would-be thieves.

Electronic security is more in-depth, and determining your specific needs may require time and research, but there are some things you can do in the meantime.

Online Security Measures:

Activate Firewalls

Antivirus Software

Encryption Programs

Strong Passwords

By employing just these basic security measures, you're already well on your way to mitigating the risk of a data breach.

Insufficient Funds

As a business owner, you'll have a great deal of control over day-to-day operations and the amount and type of projects you take on, but you can't control everything.

There's always a possibility a customer will pay late or not pay at all.

Offering automatic payment and providing written agreements and/or due date reminders is a great way to deter missed/late payments, but you can't prevent them together.

When your business coffers are well-padded, late payments aren't a big problem, and non-payment, while a headache, is remediable.

But, for new businesses without much, if any, cushioning, a delay in even a single payment can be problematic at best and catastrophic if the money is needed to pay a business debt, bill, or general expense.

To avoid finding yourself without enough money to cover the cost of doing business, consider a business line of credit. Similar to a business loan, business lines of credit have pre-determined approval criteria and can range from as little as $1,000 to more than $100,000.

With a business line of credit, you only repay/pay interest

on what you use. In other words, if you're approved for $5,000, but you only use $132, you only repay/pay interest on $132.

If you haven't been in business long enough to qualify for a business line of credit, consider having a back-up business or personal credit card that allows cash advances.

Refrain from using for anything other than emergencies. Cash advances on credit cards often come with sky-high interest rates.

Business Failure

No one wants to fail. It feels terrible, and it's embarrassing. As a business owner, the sting of failure is even worse. And there's a good chance you might fail.

Statistically, half of all new businesses fail within the first three years. Of those that survive the three-year curve, more than half will break even over the next few years. Only 30 percent of new businesses see profits before the five-year mark.

It's a stark reality, but it's one you need to face with open eyes. But don't throw the towel in just yet. Knowing the odds gives you an advantage.

If you have the determination to succeed, are willing to put in the work, and can react to curve balls with flexibility and creativity, then you have a pretty good chance of beating the odds.

Personal Financial Loss

This isn't a risk everyone faces. If you're comfortable retired, are just looking for a side gig, or if you have a trust fund, spouse, or personal fortune to fall back on, your personal finances aren't at risk. For everyone else, this is the biggest risk you face.

There's no way to know for sure if or when you'll make money or how much money you'll make. Even if you have a decent nest egg to cover your expenses until your business takes off, you have to be prepared for the possibility that it won't take off at all. Or, if it does, that it will take longer than what you planned.

If you're depending on your business to support yourself, you're taking the risk of personal financial ruin. Maybe you're already facing financial disaster or are unable to find a job, and turning things around with your own business, is your only hope of staying afloat. If that's the case, it may make sense to go all in.

But, if that's not the case, and you currently have a job, the best way to avoid the risk of personal financial ruin is to keep your job, at least until you know your business can turn a profit.

Nothing Great Comes without Risks

Luckily, when that something great happens to be owning a business, you can reduce your vulnerability to risks by following best practices for planning, establishing, and managing your business.

Chapter Two: How to Start a Business – Overview

There are a few things you need to know before you start a business. Like how to legally structure, establish and register your business to start.

This chapter covers all of that and more.

Know Thyself and Thy Market

Before starting a new business, it's a good idea to first consider what you're good at, what you enjoy doing, and what will make money. Great businesses are built when personal skills, lucrative ideas, and passion align.

If you're reading this book, chances are you know you want to start a home-based business, but you don't know which type of business you should start. We'll go over multiple options for your home business in future chapters, but for now, start thinking about the things that you do well and things you enjoy.

Ideally, your home-based business will be a labor of love, but even if it's not, its focus shouldn't be on anything you actively dislike. It doesn't bode well for the future of your dog walking business if you hate the cold and live in New York, where it's cold for a portion of the year.

Likewise, your business shouldn't be built around something in which you lack skill or talent. If you're only an average cook at best, a meal prep or personal chef business, regardless of local demand, is unlikely to succeed.

Think about what you're good at and what you enjoy as you make your way through the chapters to follow. Earmark or tag any home business ideas that involve something you're good at and enjoy doing. Your tags don't have to be precise. If you're a good cook, like dogs, know how to build websites, have a way with words, and are experienced in secretarial roles, tag all jobs associated with those key skills.

Once you've amassed a list of potential businesses, you can separate it into two groups: things you love doing and things you just like doing. Set the "like" group aside and focus first on the "love" group.

For each business idea, consider the amount of money that can be made, your skills in that area, and how much you would enjoy doing it. Then rearrange the list in ascending order, starting with the most profitable/loved/apt business idea.

When that's finished, it's time for marker research. Starting at the top, make your way down the list researching the local (or online) market for each business. For instance, if personal chef is at the top of your list. Do an internet search for personal chefs in your area. What type of results are returned?

If your search turns up lots of meal delivery or prep services but only a couple of websites for local personal chefs, you might be on to something. Before moving forward, check out their websites, noting what they offer, their prices, and how they're advertising their business. Or, if your search yields no local returns, research personal chefs in nearby areas with similar demographics.

Next, look up local demographics for your area: population size, income, education, and other data points. With this information in mind, consider what portion of the population is likely to need or want your product or service. For example, if you're offering elder care, consider what portion of the population is above age 75. Next, look at the housing situation and the average income for those people.

If there are 117,000 people over the age of 75 in your area, but only 55 percent live in traditional (non-assisted) housing, and of that 55 percent, only 45 percent have a median household income above $40,000, then your available market is about 29,000 people.

Research indicates that most successful start-ups are able to engage between one and five percent of their available market. Within the parameters of the scenario above, that means your actual market size is between 290 and 1,450 people. That may not seem like much, but if your area has an aging population of moderately wealthy people, few social programs, and just as few private elderly care businesses, you may be on to one hell of a business idea.

To sum it up, consider who your customers are, if there are enough of them, and what the competition is like before doing anything else.

Map it Out

Once you have a business idea firmly in place, map out the specifics. Determine the specific need to sell and furnish the product/service, the time required to complete each sale, and the cost of everything every step of the way. You don't want to advertise a dog walking service if you don't have enough money to zig-zag across town driving to client homes.

If you live in an area with high parking costs and unreliable public transit, you need to know in advance how long it takes to traverse between neighborhoods and what you'll need to earn per dog to cover your time, gas, and parking expenses. Likewise, if you plan to start a custom pet portrait business before you set prices, you'll need to determine the time, cost, and method of furnishing a single order.

Consider the following questions:

How much time is required to complete a portrait at each canvas size offered?

What supplies are needed to complete a portrait?

What is the cost of those supplies?

How will customers submit pictures of their pets?

What's the minimum image needed?

When will customers provide payment?

How will customers receive completed portraits?

Mapping out the process and the expected cost in advance will help you determine your prices and set deliverable deadlines down the line. Plus, when looked at as a whole, your answers to these questions are a glimpse into the future day-to-day operations of your start-up.

What's in a Name?

Once you know what type of business to start, you have to figure out what to call it. When naming a business, remember this: a clever name is great, especially if it's easy to remember and apt, but it's not everything.

Ideally, you'll come up with a clever name that describes who you are and what you do, but if that doesn't happen, don't let obsessing over it stall your process. The most important thing when coming up with a name is landing on one that is easy to remember and easy to relay.

Marketing professionals recommend keeping business names short, pronounceable, easily spelled, and as descriptive as possible. But that's easier said than done. Keep a running list of potential names. Jot down anything that comes to mind and once you have a couple dozen, begin narrowing it down to your top few picks.

Starting with your favorites, check the availability of names. First, search the name in your state's business entity registry. If it's available, see if it's trademarked by searching the U.S. Patent and Trademark Office website. (www.uspto.gov).

Next, check to see if it is available as a domain using the Internet Corporation for Assigned Names and Numbers, or ICANN's, domain registry look-up tool. It's not uncommon to discover your favorite names are all already someone else's domain. If you're favorite are out of the running, come up with a few easy and apt backups, like "Frank's Taco Sauce" or "Sasha Accounting Services."

Finally, remember you're don't have to have the perfect

name to launch; you just have to have one that's good
enough. You can always change it in the future.

Making it Official

Before you file for a business license, you need to
determine the financial structure of your business.

Since you're reading this book, you're looking for a low-
cost, easy-to-start home business. This gives you three
options: Sole Proprietorship (SP), Limited Liability
Corporation (LLC), or if you plan on going into business
with one or more other people, a Partnership Trust (PT).

Sole Proprietorships are the simplest type of business to
form. They're unincorporated pass-through entities owned
by a single person who reports profits and losses on their
individual tax return.

The perks of a sole proprietorship are ease of registration,
limited paperwork, and low cost. The cons are liability
and risk. As the owner of a sole-proprietorship, you're
personally liable in lawsuits against your business. If
you're sued and lose, your personal assets are on the line.

Your home, car, bank accounts, etc., can be seized to cover damages. This is true regardless of how or when you received or purchased the asset in question.

In all honestly, forming an LLC is the best option. LLCs are hybrid organizations designed with small businesses in mind. They offer much of the protections of incorporation, but they're easier to register and have a lower price tag.

LLCs are pass-through entities where profits are passed directly through to the owner and taxed at the owner/shareholder level unless purposely structured otherwise. They also limit liability, which means if you're sued, only your business assets are at risk of seizure.

Partnership Trusts are unincorporated pass-through entities owned by two or more people who split profits and report them on their individual tax returns. They're basically the same as a sole proprietorship, but for more than one person.

Like with an SP, with a PT, if the company is sued, the personal assets of all partners are on the line. This is true for investing partners as well as managing partners.

Let's say your cousin gives you enough money to start a business in exchange for a 40 percent stake in the company, but make all the decisions and run day-to-day operations. If the business is sued, your personal assets and your cousin's personal assets risk seizure.

Forming an LLC

As previously mentioned, forming an LLC requires more paperwork and has a higher cost than an SP or PT, but forming one isn't all that difficult. And the slightly higher cost equates to significantly better protection.

The most expensive part of the process is hiring legal counsel, which isn't technically required, but experts do recommend at least hiring a lawyer to review your paperwork.

The process of forming an LLC can be broken down into six steps, and by the time you're ready to do it, you'll have already completed the first step.

LLC Formation:

Step 1: Pick a name for your business

Step 2: Choose a registered agent

Step 3: File incorporation paperwork with your state

Step 4: File an Operating Agreement with your state

Step 5: Obtain an EIN from the IRS

Step 6: Apply for a local/state business license

Registered Agent

A registered agent is just someone who agrees to accept legal documents on behalf of your business Monday through Friday during normal business hours, with the exception of holidays.

You can be your business' registered agent, but because of the off chance that you'll end up getting sued and could then be served while meeting with a client, most business owners choose a close friend or family member or hire a registered agent business.

Articles of Incorporation and Operating Agreements

Thinking about writing Articles of Incorporation and an Operating Agreement is probably worse than actually doing it. There are dozens of free and low-cost Articles of Incorporation templates online. All you need to do is download one and customize it for your business.

Most states post detailed information on exactly what your Operating Agreement needs to include. The hardest part might be determining which state agency posts it. If you can't find it, call your local branch of the Small Business Administration for assistance.

EIN

The IRS might not be your cup of tea, but you'll need to go through this agency to obtain an EIN or Employer Identification Number. An EIN is basically a social security number for your business, which you'll need come tax time, as well as business loans, lines of credit, grants, and contracts.

You can apply for an EIN on the IRS website (www.irs.gov) or by downloading an SS-4 form and mailing it to the IRS. (https://www.irs.gov/pub/irs-pdf/fss4.pdf)

General Establishment Costs

The cost of local and state licenses and permits varies by city and state. The average cost of a business license is about $75-$100, but in some areas, a business license will cost about $200-$250. Your municipality may or may not require you to obtain a business permit. These tend to cost between $50-$150, plus a processing fee of $25. Registering your business with the IRS, which you'll need to do to obtain an EIN, is $75. In most areas, obtaining a DBA will cost between $20-$50. And LLC filing fees range between $50-$150 in most states.

It's rare for a small business start-up to have to contend with all the fees listed above right at the onset, and you can hold-off on certain aspects of establishment for a short-period of time without putting yourself and your business in legal jeopardy.

And you can hold off on obtaining an EIN until you've earned $400 in profit (after costs). If you're on a tight budget, waiting a couple months to incorporate or file for an EIN provides the freedom to focus that money elsewhere for a short period of time.

Bank on It

As a business owner, it's important that your personal financial transactions are kept separate from your business' financial transactions. In other words, unless you're just dipping your toe in the water, you don't want to accept payments for services or products in your personal name. You should have a separate business banking ledger and account.

This doesn't mean you have to open a business banking account, though you should consider it. But you should open a bank account in your business' name. You can do this by filing for a DBA, which stands for doing business as, with your local county government. DBAs don't cost much, and they are a useful tool for a new small business owner, as they make it legal to conduct business under a different name than your legal name.

In other words, they enable you to open accounts, enter into contracts and accept payments made to your business. If you're considering opening a business banking account, make sure to do your homework first. Deciding which bank and type of business account to go with can be a bit tricky.

To make it easier, jot down what you want from your bank, such as nearby no-fee ATMs, local branches, the ability to access a business line of credit, etc., then search local banks to see which ones offer the features you need. Compare the interest rates and fees charged at each of these banks to determine the best option.

Building an Online Presence

Websites are integral to the success of many home-based businesses. Your website is the first selling point for many customers. It should be professional, functional, easy to navigate, and kept up-to-date. Professional websites have clean layouts, utilize modern fonts, and limit content unrelated to the business to the occasional background story on the "about us" or "our history" page.

A functional website doesn't have to have advanced functioning capabilities, but it has to work. This means links that are active and route to their indicated destination. And working functions were advertised. For instance, if you offer online purchases/payments, that function needs to work.

Navigational ease means users can find the information they are looking for quickly and without inside knowledge of the site's layout. Up-to-date websites contain current pricing/products/services. In other words, if you no longer offer a certain service, your website should not list it as a service offered.

Most domain names come with annual registration fees of between $5-$20 and usually come with the option to buy a three-year package at a reduced rate. Building a website for that domain name is a bit more expensive. Hiring a professional website designer is pricey, and for anyone working under a tight budget or just curious to see if they're able to bring money in on the side doing something they enjoy, it's pretty much out of the question.

If you know someone who can help you build a website, consider asking for a favor or a trade. If you don't know a website designer, don't worry. There are options available for those on a tight budget with little-to-no website design experience.

For those with some experience, platforms like WordPress offer free and low-cost templates, and if you limit paid plug-ins, you can keep your costs down to about $11 per month, plus $12 annually for your domain name. For those without experience, consider Google Sites or Wix.

The layouts on Google Sites aren't stunning, but the ones featured in the business section are professional, and you don't have to have any previous experience to use the platform. Building in Google Sites is as easy as filling in content in a word layout.

Google charges a $6 monthly fee to use your domain name on their platform. However, there's a short-term workaround for this. You can redirect your domain URL to the website URL. This is done on the site where you purchased your domain name. Log into your account; go to the Domains section and select "manage"; then look for domain forwarding; click "add new" and enter your Google Sites URL. This way, you can get your business cards printed with your domain name, and when someone types it in, they will be redirected to your free Google Sites website.

However, keep in mind that they are being redirected, which means once they arrive at your Google Sites website, the actual URL in the URL bar. It's a decent way to save money in the short-run, but it shouldn't be a permanent solution.

Wix is another great option for people with no experience building websites. It's easy to use, and while slightly more expensive than Google Sites, it offers a collection of stunning professional templates.

Wix offers eight packages. The cheapest is $13 per month for a site with your personal domain. This option will work for a few home businesses, but for most, the $17 per month entrepreneurs and freelancers' package or the $22 pro package offer more bang for your buck. The pro package even comes with professional logo design and visitor analytics, and site booster apps.

Finally, one additional option is to forgo a website altogether and opt instead for a Facebook business page. While doing this might work in the short-term, it isn't a good idea for long-term marketing and online presence building.

Once you're marketing to the general public, your website is an essential tool in forming a brand, informing customers, and establishing professionalism. Plus, not everyone uses Facebook.

If you do opt for a Facebook business page in lieu of a website, remember you'll have to print new business cards, labels, letterhead, etc., with your website URL when you get one.

It's better to secure your domain name early and get something up, even if it's just a well-designed landing page with a link to your Facebook page and/or your phone number and order hours. You can always expand on it or update it later.

Check out websites like Fiverr for low-cost assistance building a landing page. Or post an ad in the gigs section on craigslist that explaining your needs and budget.

Chapter Three: Getting the Word Out

You found the home business that's perfect for you; made it official; bought a domain name; and built a website. Now what? Unless you already have a cohort of customers, it's time to get the word out. There are a few ways to do this.

You can advertise your business in local papers or online, market it on social media or in person, post flyers around town, or list your wares/services on any number of websites. You can also peruse local and online listings and apply for gigs or submit proposals.

The specific type of advertising/marketing that's best for your business depends on what type of business you have. For ideas related to your particular business, check out the How to Sell It section under each home business.

Remember, each business is unique, and what works for some may not work for others. Try out as many forms of advertising and marketing as you desire; just make sure to track results to determine which form yields the best results.

Ways to get the word out:

Print Media

Broadcast Media

Digital Media

Social Media

Print Materials

Networking

Giving Back to Get Back

Print Media

When it comes to print media, you have a few options.
You can pay for a traditional advertisement in a local
paper or magazine; spend a few dollars in the classifieds,
or try to get free coverage through the distribution of a
press release.

Obviously, free coverage sounds like the best option, and
if you can wing it, it definitely is, but unless you're a big
fish in a small pond; have an in with a reporter; or your
local paper regularly writes about home-based businesses,
getting print coverage isn't easy.

To do it, your business needs to be not just note-worthy
but news-worthy. Are you offering a product or service
there is a desperate need for in your town? Did you

stumble upon a turquoise mine in your backyard and are making it into jewelry? Is there a harrowing story behind your great-grandmother's banana-nut bread recipe? It's all about finding a compelling angle. If you have one, you just might score some precious print real estate free of charge.

Once you've determined your angle, you'll need to reach out to the right reporters. The story of your ancestral banana-nut bread isn't exactly front-page material for most papers, but it might just make the front of the home or lifestyle section. Figure out who to contact, then read a couple of their past articles before reaching out to them. Reporters are people like everyone else, and it feels good to have their work acknowledged.

You can reach out by phone or text or both, but remember, more often than not, they field "sales-like pitches" on a daily basis. The goal is to be persistent but not over-bearing. Once you reach them, authenticity is key. Reporters don't want to be sold a story, so avoid using superficial or aggressive language. Remember, you're engaging them with a story — your story.

Even if they decline to write about it, keep it friendly. Let them know you understand and look forward to continuing to follow their work. Thank them for their time and politely end the call. Like it or not, reporters, even the ones that seem to barely mask a personal bias, are better off as friends than enemies. And, the truth is, most of them, especially in the print world, really do strive to offer truthful and accurate content. So even if you feel like they snubbed you, especially if you feel like they snubbed you, be polite.

It's not that some reporter will set out to ruin your business if you're not, but the truth is there are slow news weeks, and most reporters keep a file of potential stories to pursue on those weeks. If you're rude, you won't make it to the backup file. And you're less likely to be quoted and mentioned in future articles, should an incidental mention of you/your business be possible down the line.

When covering community events, reporters often take stock of familiar, friendly faces while on the lookout for quotes about the event. A good reporter will gather said quotes from a mix of new faces and a different assortment of familiar ones at each event he or she covers. It's a good idea to be one of those friendly, familiar ones.

If you're an introvert, you probably detest the ideas of cold calling a reporter or approaching one to chit-chat at an event. I hear you. You still might have to brave a phone call at some point, but you avoid it for now by issuing a press release. If you're going to go the route of the press release, start by making a list of reporters to distribute it to, then do a little research on the proper format and AP Style.

Reporters get dozens of press releases each day, and a quick way to weed through them is to toss out any that have bush-league formatting. Brief yourself on the correct AP format for datelines, capitalization, and general grammar. And, if you can, get someone to give it a quick read-through before distributing it.

The best time to send a press release is mid-morning. By lunchtime, most reporters are out getting a story or hard at work writing one. The goal is for it to reach them after they've had their morning coffee while they are still planning their stories for the day/week.

Wait 36-48 hours after distribution, then shoot out a follow-up email to make sure they received it. Most of the time, this won't be make or break, but every once in a while, a story falls through, and a follow-up call/email seals the deal on what will replace it.

As mentioned at the top of this section, there are two other methods for marketing print — paid advertisements and classified ads. Paid advertisements can be pricey, especially if you're looking to do it in a glossy mag.

Prices vary based on the publication, location, size of the ad, placement of the ad, and if it runs in color or black and white. The decision of whether or not it's worth it boils down to knowing your market and being able to afford it.

Print media isn't as popular as it once was, but despite its decline, recent studies indicate that print media marketing still has a high return on investment (ROI). Businesses that embarked on narrowly target print media marketing campaigns had an average ROI of 120 percent in one study.

In other words, if successful, you would earn back everything you spent, plus 20 percent. However, these studies track major advertising campaigns from businesses that can dedicate a full team of professionals to skillfully crafting and expertly placing their ads. It's worth looking into, but if the cost doesn't click, consider alternative methods of marketing.

Finally, there are the classifieds. These one-inch ads don't really sparkle, but depending on who you're marketing to, they might just do the trick. Rates vary, but unless you're putting one in a major publication like the New York Times, which will set you back a few hundred dollars, these mini-ads usually run around $20-$40. Still, it's $20-$40 wasted if the general readership isn't your target customer. Before buying any ad space, no matter how cheap, find out if doing so has the potential to get your business in front of potential customers.

Broadcast Media

This definitely isn't the cheapest method of advertisement. Not only do you have to pay for air space, but also to develop a high-quality ad that will capture the attention of viewers and listeners. The effectiveness of TV advertisement is on the decline, but in general, the plus side of shelling out between $1,000-$5,000 for a local commercial and upwards of $30,000 for a national commercial is that it is supposed to reach a captive audience. And, if it does, that's great. But personally, I wouldn't bet on it. How many people do you know that sit through commercials (or, for that matter, still pay for cable)?

The majority of Gen Xers, as well as most Millennials, prefer streaming services to cable. If you're marketing to Boomers, there's a chance your ad will be seen and heard. But remember, just because many Boomers still pay for cable, it doesn't mean they watch commercials. In my experience, most people channel surf, hit mute, or get up to do something else while commercials air.

On the other hand, advertising on TV does have some advantages. It reaches a wide yet targeted audience. It allows you to both say and show what you do. And, when done well, commercials can cultivate brand loyalty, stir up feelings and create a sense of need in viewers.

If a TV ad is out of your budget, there are always radio ads. Radio ads are significantly less expensive and much easier to produce. The cost to air a radio ad depends on where you live, what time it is, and who listens to that station. Stations that cater primarily to people between the ages of 25-55 will charge higher rates than stations with younger or older listeners; morning and evening commute blocks cost more than midday and late-night blocks, and the more people listening/reached, the higher the cost.

In general, radio advertisements run between $199-$4,999 per week for daily runs. And, for some businesses, they're a low-cost, direct line to a ready customer base. Radio ads don't work for every business. The more niche your product or service, the less likely you are to see a return on your investment. The companies that report the highest returns (114 to 117 percent) on radio ads predominately fall into one of the following categories: department store, telecommunications provider, mass merchandiser; chain restaurant; or home improvement center.

If you have the skills to produce your own radio ad and

you can get a good rate for peak air time, it might be worth considering. While you're considering that, also consider who will be reached if you ran the same ad on a streaming service like Pandora.

Digital Media

Unless you're targeting the elderly or your local area lacks quality internet access, you may want to think about digital ads, which cost less and can be more specifically targeted to your market base. There are multiple types of digital ads and a seemingly endless number of sites that display ads. Determining where to place your ad and which type of ad to places comes back to knowing your ideal customer.

Who do you imagine buying your product or service? What's their age group? What type of places do they work? Get to know your ideal customer, and you can figure out the best places to reach them online.

Facebook is still pretty popular, but if you're marketing to college students, you may be better off on Instagram, TikTok, or any number of other social media sites, like

YouTube, which has users from every generation.

There are about seven mainstream forms of digital advertising. They include:

Display Ads

Retargeting

Search Engine

Native Advertising

Content Marketing

Email Marketing

Display Ads

Display ads are paid online advertisements that usually include an image and limited text and appear in website banners and sidebars, as pop-ups, and as landing pages. The biggest benefit to this type of digital media advertising is the ability to specifically target potential customers and, if they click, take them directly to your website or a landing page/sales funnel.

The downside is most people don't click on display ads. And ad blocking software may prevent potential customers from even seeing your ad.

Retargeting

On the other hand, when coupled with retargeting, display ads are surprisingly successful. Retargeting uses cookies to follow potential customers around the web and display ads for your business on other websites and in search results. It seems a little invasive, and perhaps it is, but marketing and advertising professionals swear by it, and studies show it is surprisingly effective.

On average, about 72 percent of online shoppers abandon their cart without making a purchase, and only eight percent return to make the purchase later. Enter retargeting, and that number of shoppers who return to purchase increases to 26 percent.

Not only does retargeting have an effect on shoppers, but it also increases the frequency with which people search for a business following an encounter with a display ad from 27 percent to 49 percent.

According to industry professionals, the secret to getting a 200 plus percent ROI is in deploying the holy trifecta of online advertising: display, retargeting, and search engine ads.

Search Engine

Search engine advertising places text ads to the side of or above search engine results when the words searched match the advertisers chosen keywords. Search advertising doesn't have a flat rate; instead, the advertiser pays for each click the ad garnishes.

In a study on the relationship between display ads and search queries, it was discovered that only 27 percent of Internet users respond to display ads by searching for the product or service on the spot. About 22 percent of people will search for a product/service from a display ad in the two weeks following when they saw it. When that happens, you want to be at the top of the results, which is where a search ad will place you.

And, if that's not enough to convince you of their ability to increase site visits and sales, consider the following:

The vast majority of site traffic is generated by search ads, is specific to the search ad. More specifically, 89 percent of traffic is not replaced with organic clicks when search ads are paused.

Internet users rarely make it to the second page of search results — 98 percent of people click on a link on the first page of results.

On average, businesses report making $2 for every $1 spent on search ads, which is an ROI of 200 percent.

Search, display, and retargeting ads are powerful tools, but when it comes to getting the word out online, they account for just one slice in the possibility pie. An equally sizable slice of that pie is made up of native ads and content marketing.

Native Ads

Native advertisements are paid ads that seamlessly blend into the media that surrounds them. You see them all the time. They appear on your Facebook feed, at the very top of Google search results pages, and as "recommend" or "sponsored articles" on news media and content-based websites.

Content Marketing

Content marketing is the development of multiple forms of digital content — articles, videos, blogs, social media posts, etc. — that don't specifically advertise your business but are designed to increase interest in the products or services you offer. In addition to the above-mentioned formats, content marketing also includes infographics, case studies, white papers, eBooks, templates, checklists, webinars, quizzes, questionnaires, downloadable guides, and more.

The idea of content marketing is multi-tiered. The first tier raises interest in your product or service and solidifies your business as the go-to locally or across an industry.

Blogs, social media posts, and infographics increase interest and brand awareness. They engage the reader/viewer. Once engaged, the second-tier goal of content marketing is to generate leads. This is usually done with the offer of free content.

That's where eBooks, checklists, templates, webinars, and other curated content comes in. Accessing the content leads to the second stage of the marketing funnel. Here, one of two things usually happens.

The potential future customer is redirected to a landing page where they can download the content and are presented with a very-limited-time, hard-to-turn-down offer. Or, in exchange for providing their email address, which will later be used to email offers, the potential customer can access the free download.

Engagement is at the top of the funnel, capturing the widest audience. Lead generation is the mid-point. And, at the bottom of the funnel is the conversion of leads to paid purchases/memberships.

Email Marketing

Email marketing is the use of email to promote your business, cultivate new customer relationships and strengthen existing customer relationships. There is a variety of software available to assist in, automate, manage and analyze email marketing effectiveness.

For small businesses and start-ups, Constant Contact is considered one of the best options. Mailer Lite is considered the easiest to use and overall cheapest; however, it lacks many of the capabilities that make its competition so popular. Drip is favored by E-Commerce businesses. Content creators recommend Convert Kit for bloggers, graphic designers, and writers in the industry. There are literally dozens of other mail managers on the market, each with its own qualities and disadvantages.

Social Media

The queen bee of digital marketing/advertisement is social media. There are dozens of marketing methods specific to social media, plus the option of paid ads. For new businesses with a limited budget, it's a great place to start getting the word out.

Social media marketing can cost as little as nothing and can make a big difference in your bottom line. The benefits range from creating brand awareness (letting people know your business is out there and the product or service you offer) to providing insight into the needs, wants, and desires of current and potential customers.

Other benefits include:

Increased Website Traffic

Geo-targeting

Relationship Building

Lead Conversion

Improvement to Search Engine Ranking

Enhanced Brand Authority

Insights into Industry Trends

Better Customer Service

Another benefit of social media marketing is its ability to humanize your company. Companies that are active on social media are also seen as more relatable, which increases customer trust and connectedness. On top of all that, it's also easy to track through built-in metrics on each platform. You can analyze the reach and success of a Facebook marketing campaign by looking at page likes, post reach, organic likes, shares, unlike, and more.

Facebook, Twitter, Instagram, Pinterest, LinkedIn, YouTube, and Google+ all provide users with a variety of metrics to analyze the success of every single post. The words used to describe specific measurements and what exactly is being measured vary from one platform to the next but understanding what each means and methods for analyzing the data provided isn't overly taxing.

Experts recommend, new businesses start with no more than two (three, if you're already familiar with this type of brand building) social media pages and focus their attention on image consistency, content reliability, growing brand awareness, and building relationships before expanding to other platforms.

Before you start building a business page/account on your personal preferred site, think about the platforms that provide the best access to your target customer. If you're marketing to active, retired women, Facebook and Pinterest will provide a wider audience than LinkedIn and Twitter. Conversely, if you're looking to market to specific professions or just professionals in general, LinkedIn should be your first stop.

After you decide which platform best reaches your target audience, consider which type of content will do the same (blogs, written posts, graphics, video, etc.). Then outline the core message you're trying to get out there, which will underlie each piece of content you develop. Next, determine a plan for consistently posting content and ensuring timely responses/interactions. Posting consistency and response time are critical in the early stages of brand building.

Starting a business is time-consuming enough on its own,

and it can be tempting to put social media on the back burner, but if your aim is to build awareness and brand authority, an erratic posting schedule, lack of engagement, and delayed responses will do more harm than help.

Brand authority establishes you as an expert in your field and your business as the go-to place to receive a particular product or service. To help ensure your ability to post regularly, consider generating a handful of non-time-specific ready-to-go posts that you can use as needed when you do not have time to generate new content.

Side note: some of the email management programs out there allow you to preschedule content and have the ability to post to your social media account/s. The real fun of social media marketing comes once you've established yourself/business and built a steady following. That's when you can deploy creative social media marketing campaigns and start reeling in real results.

If you're not the creative type, finding ideas for and guidance on unique and engaging social media marketing campaigns isn't difficult. Spend five minutes perusing the internet, and you'll be inundated with social media marketing campaign ideas for every skill level and platform.

You don't have to start with something that's never been done before. There are many tried-and-true (and fun) social media marketing strategies that lead to an increase in followers/reach, improved customer/follower relationships, lead generation, and sales.

One of the easiest is simply sharing/repining/reposting follower content that is symbiotic with your brand. Requiring more pre-planning but not-too-difficult to administer is the social media contest.

Determine what you'll give to the winner and how people will submit entries, then post the prize, rules, terms, and conditions (search and download a free T&C template to save time) and a point of contact in an eye-catching post.

To reap the promotional benefits of this campaign, contest entry should be something that's fun yet promotes your business. Think reposts, hashtags, short videos that include your product, etc.

Other simple marketing strategies include how-to videos, hosting a Q&A, making a meme, polling your audience, allowing a customer to take over your feed for 24 hours, finding fun yet an on-message way to participate in Throwback Thursday, and recommending products/services, to name a few.

Here your imagination is the limit. You can keep it simple or do something that will set the internet ablaze. But, whatever you do, make sure it's on-brand with your brand.

Print Materials

It's easy to overlook the importance of having business cards when you first start out, but the truth is marketing starts with your business card. Order a set on day one and get in the habit of carrying them with you. You never know when a casual conversation will end in a request for one, and not having them (or not having them on you) can result in the loss of a sale or business opportunity.

A well-designed, professionally printed, and concise business card establishes credibility and professionalism and helps people remember you. There are no steadfast rules on style — you can opt for a standard card, one with a unique feel or shape, or a trifold — but keep the design on-brand with your business and make sure to include all important information.

Must-Have Information:

Your Name

Business Logo

Website URL

Phone Number

Email Address

If there is room, you can also include a brief description of what you specialize in and the products or services offered. If customers are coming to your home, you may also want to include a street address, hours, and if walk-ins are permitted or appointments are required.

Home-printed cards are no substitution for the real thing, and with the low-cost options offered by many professional printing services, procuring quality cards won't eat up much of your budget.

Request proof from the printer before ordering a full set of cards. Once it arrives and you confirm it's what you want, all you have to do is approve the design, pick the quantity and place an order.

Informative brochures can also make for a powerful marketing tool when meeting with prospective clients, working at trade shows, or networking with industry peers.

When designing informational brochures, stay on brand by using a similar or complementary style as the one you chose for your business cards and making sure your messaging is consistent with your messaging elsewhere.

Always keep your target customer in mind. Especially when creating print content.

Fancy card stock is great if your ideal clients are business moguls or successful stockbrokers, but if you're aiming for a budget-conscious crowd, consider a simpler look and feel.

Often people make snap judgments on businesses based on the quality and design of their brochures. Clean, professional designs that highlight your services and specialty are best.

That doesn't mean you can't include photos of your product or service; a photo of yourself with a brief bio; client reviews or testimonials; or infographics that showcase noteworthy stats/information.

Nor does it mean minimalist. It just means not over-burdened by design or over-crowded with information.

Brochures are great to have on hand at networking events and trade shows, but you can utilize them elsewhere too. Schedule times to meet with professionals in related industries.

For example, if you're starting a dog-walking business, introduce yourself to local groomers, independent pet supply store owners, animal trainers, boarding facilities, and maybe even local veterinary clinics.

See if they are interested in swapping cards/brochures. You leave some of yours for their clients and take some of theirs to have on hand for your clients.

In addition to related businesses, you can request permission to leave your brochures at a variety of community establishments, such as local churches, travel information centers, college campuses, recreational areas, civic centers, etc.

Depending on your business, you may also want to consider flyers. The nice thing about flyers is they are easy for both you and the potential customer, who only has to snap a pic or jot down a phone number or URL to get more information later.

For flyers to work, they have to check three boxes:

Style: A well-designed, visually captivating image or clever wording to grab the attention of and linger on in the mind of the viewer.

Distribution: Places where your target customers live, work, eat, play, or regularly traverse.

Location: Places related to or complementary to the service or product you offer. (For the dog walking business, this might be a local dog park or pet-friendly apartment buildings.)

With the exception of the business card, which all business owners should have, print material marketing yields the best results when used by local businesses servicing a specific geographic area when engaging prospective clients; and when participating in networking events or trade shows.

Networking

One of the best ways to get the word out about your new business is to go out. Meet people. Attend events. Join a club.

When the mood is right, strike up casual conversations with the person in line behind you or while waiting for the subway. Get to know the people in your daily life, like your barista or doorman, with whom you normally only exchange pleasantries.

Networking isn't about the perfect sales pitch or making deals; it's about meeting people. Successful networking builds relationships and enhances your understanding of your industry or local area, and provides an opportunity for you to discover ways to improve your business.

The leads and sales generated by networking are a positive side-effect. And there's more where that came from. By getting out there and socializing, you'll meet talented professionals from industries outside your own, who you can reach out to down the line when you're redesigning your website or filing taxes.

Consider joining your local chamber of commerce or attending business seminars and other events that will allow you to meet fellow business owners and industry leaders. Use these events to grow professionally and build relationships.

That's not to say you shouldn't talk about what you do. You absolutely should. But don't approach it as a sales pitch.

Bring your business cards and freely offer one up when you meet someone you want to connect with later or who might be a potential client. It might surprise you to discover just how many leads, recommendations, and clients you can gain through genuine expressions of interest in other people.

Give Back to Get Back

There's a reason why we donate to worthy causes and volunteer our time with charities. Giving back feels good. And, as a business owner, when you give back, you not only get to feel good, but you also get something back in return. If you want to expand awareness of your business and generate new leads, consider volunteering.

The product or service you specialize in can help aid in the mission of a non-profit, help raise funds for a charity or assist a local group in putting on an annual event. It doesn't matter what type of business you have; chances are your skills, services, or products can be levied for a good cause. Book-keeping services can be auctioned, home-made soaps can be added to gala loot bags, and marketing expertise can be a boon for local fundraising efforts.

Owners of e-commerce businesses can teach workshops. Wood-workers can build sets. Caterers can cater annual fundraising dinners. Think about the local organizations that could benefit from your skills, services, products, or expertise.

Locally-based organizations and charities work just as hard as their larger counterparts. They just do it on a smaller scale, which means they're working with fewer resources and fewer restrictions. And that's good news for small businesses, like yours.

There's nothing wrong with offering to help in a way that will also be helpful to you. For example, if you're a graphic designer, rather than offer your services point-blank, offer to design the program for an annual charity auction or the shirts for the annual 5K.

In exchange for your time and quality work, request your business be recognized in the program or having your logo on the shirt.

By lending a hand in these ways, your business exposure will extend not only to members/employees/volunteers within the organization but outside the organization to the general public. It's a great way to get your name out there, grow brand recognition and showcase your skills.

Before making offers or accepting requests for your goods or services, determine the value it will bring to your business. Imagine you're a website designer fielding two separate requests for assistance but can only honor one. The size and general scope of both jobs are the same. One is from a local booster club tasked with planning the high school senior class trip. The other is to build a relatively simple website for a local charity.

While the amount of work is the same for both projects, one website is pretty much guaranteed to get a lot of traffic and mentions/links on social media by excited soon-to-be-graduates for a period of six-months preceding and two months following the event as traffic winds down to none.

The other will be the permanent website, which will see a spike in traffic and new visits in the weeks preceding each of three annual events, but new activity stagnates outside those windows of time.

The social media mentions from the senior trip website are great in the short run but don't offer the same potential for enhancing brand recognition and generating leads over time as the charity's website.

Plus, the traffic generated on the charity site comes from consumers with more purchasing power and is probably the better option. It doesn't hurt to ask for the recognition you want to receive.

In the above scenario, proper recognition might include a link to your business on the website, mention of your business in a press release about the launch of the new site, recognition in the program for the annual year-end fundraiser, a ticket to said fundraiser, and donor mention at the fundraiser.

Volunteering feels great, and it can make a big difference in your community or towards a cause you believe in. And it can help grow your business and establish you as an expert in your field.

Final Thoughts on Advertising

There are a variety of other ways to get the word out — billboards, direct mail, promotional stunts — any one of which may work best for your business. The aim of this section was to cover methods popular with small business owners and applicable across multiple fields.

Occasionally certain marketing and advertising methods are particularly advantageous to specific business types; when this is the case, it will be covered in more detail in the section for that business.

Chapter Four: Tips and Tricks

Phone Photography

Today's phones have fantastic cameras, capable of capturing breath-taking, high-resolution images, but just because they're capable of it doesn't mean they always do it. To improve your odds of snapping the perfect pic for your website, social media feed, or other business needs, consider some of the following tips for phone photography.

1. Place your product on a flat surface with a white or grey background. Consider using rolled seamless-paper or ironed fabric. Make sure there are no creases or dents in the paper or cloth.

2. Consider purchasing or borrowing a tripod or stand to enhance clarity, especially in less than ideal lighting situations. Prices for phone tripods range from $5-$30.

3. If your photos still lack sharpness or need to be taken in low-light situations, consider purchasing a wireless remote for mobile photography. They're usually less than $10.

4. Soft, natural, and in-direct lighting is usually best. Add artificial lighting where needed to remove shadows or use a bounce board to redirect light.

5. For product/food photography, consider making a lightbox. Directions on how to do so follow this section and can be found by searching "easy DIY lightbox" in your internet browser of choice.

6. Turn on gridlines to balance the composition.

Remember, the focus of your image should be in the center box of the grid. To turn on gridlines, go to settings, then camera, then toggle the button-marked grid to the on position for iPhones. For Androids, go to settings and scroll down until you see "grid lines," then tap the switch to the on position.

7. Avoid zooming in, using flash, or shooting with a filter.

8. Consider downloading a camera app for enhanced features. Research and read reviews before you buy.

9. If shooting outdoors in harsh lighting, shoot through the clean and scratch-free lens of a pair of sunglasses.

DIY Light Box Directions

You can make your own lightbox for product and food photography using things you probably have lying around the house.

Supplies:

Cardboard box

Precision knife or box cutter

Ruler

White, low-shine paper size A3 or poster board

White paper, parchment paper, or thin fabric

Tape

Two desk lamps

Two light bulbs (bulbs with similar color and wattage
work best)

Step 1: Remove flaps from the top of the box, then place
the box on a sturdy surface with an opening facing toward
you.

Step 2: Using your ruler and pencil, trace a window with
a one-inch border on the right side of the box.

Step 3: Cut out the window.

Step 4: Repeat steps two and three on the left side of the box.

Step 5: Cut a piece of poster board or A-3 paper to the width of your box. It should be long enough to cover the bottom, back, and top of the interior, with about a half-inch tab at each end to secure the outer top and bottom of the box.

Step 6: Place the paper in your box and secure it in place by taping one end to the outside top of your box and the other end to the outside bottom of your box.

Step 7: Cover the windows on each side of your box with low-shine white paper, parchment paper, or fabric. If using fabric, iron first to remove wrinkles. Pull the paper tight across the window, then secure it in place with tape on each end. Then, repeat with the other window.

Step 8: Place one desk lamp on each side of your box so that the light of each shines through the window on the same side.

Step 9: Place your product inside the box and take a picture. Move the lights around as needed, or experiment with different papers/fabrics/lighting until you get the look you want.

Logo Design

The following websites feature logo design services:

https://www.logomyway.com/logo-maker/

https://www.fiverr.com/?source=top_nav

https://www.logogenie.net/create-low-budget-logo

https://www.logoglo.com/#top

https://99designs.com

https://www.brandcrowd.com/maker/tag/cheap

Chapter Five: Jobs for the Kitchen Wizard

Do you know your way around the kitchen? Do your dishes runout first at potlucks? Can you make a meal in a pinch out of seemingly random ingredients? Prepare a feast on a budget? Host a dinner party with one day's notice?

If you answered yes to two or more of the above questions, you're a kitchen wizard, and you just might find the perfect home business in this chapter.

Pros and Cons

Pros:

You'll be doing something you enjoy

You're your own boss

Low start-up costs

Cons:

You have to stay on top of state and local food or feed laws and regulations

When ingredients are not used and replaced regularly, cookies suffer

You must be vigilant about allergen contamination and food safety standards

It can take a while to build a solid customer base

Getting Started

Step One: Food safety laws vary from state to state; before you sell food to anyone, you need to know your state's laws. Some states require food licensing, put a cap on the total dollar amount of sales annually, require an annual health inspection, and/or require food for sale to the public to be prepared in a separate kitchen.

For example, in Michigan, the Cottage Foods Law allows people to sell baked goods and specific other foods prepared in their home without a food license or being subject to a health inspection.

In Illinois, the Home Kitchen Operations Law allows people to sell baked goods made in their home without an inspection or food license but puts a $1,000 cap on sales per month, and in order to be covered under the law, their county government must first pass an ordinance allowing it.

In regard to other food items, food service insurance and/or a food service permit may be required. Even if insurance is required in your area, experts recommend you get it. The average cost for food start-ups is only $40 a month. Where required, food service permits often include an inspection and cost $100-$200.

Dog treats or feed regulation information is available from the Association of American Feed Control Officials (AAFCO). Their website features a helpful "Find Your State Feed Control Official" page that details requirements, costs, and more for all states and territories in North America.

The AAFCO Pet Food and Treat Label Requirements and the FDA at a Glance: Final Rule on Preventative Control for Animal Food are helpful resources for dog biscuit start-ups.

Step Two: Come up with a name for your business and check to see if it is available. We have previously examined how to come up with a name.

Step Three: Make it official. Determine how you want to structure your business, file the forms needed, register a domain name and make it official.

Step Four: Apply for city/county required permits and licenses.

Step Five: Collect and build media. Take pictures of your work. They don't need to be of professional quality. At this point, all you need to capture a few quality pics are a smartphone, good lighting, and a steady hand.

Indoor pictures can be tricky, though. Take pictures in a place with plenty of natural light. If that's not possible, consider bulbs that give off white or natural hues.

Make sure your wares and experiment with different set-ups. Switch out plates and racks, see how different backgrounds affect the image, and try different food arrangements.

Snap away. It's better to have too many pictures than too little. You can narrow them down later.

Step Six: Create a logo.

Step Seven: Determine your costs and prices. (See specific sections for more information.)

Step Eight: Build a website.

Step Nine: Order print materials and packaging. Buy Ingredients.

Step Ten: Do a test run.

The Gourmet Cookie Business

Business Description

If you enjoy making cookies and can make picture-perfect trays time after time, this home business could be a labor of love. The specific types of cookies you offer are up to you. All you have to do is fulfill website/phone orders as they come in and get them to paying customers.

This business requires you to be a quality baker; stay up-to-date on local/state health code and food regulations; coordinate bake-times, quantities, and equipment for multiple orders; keep track of orders and payments, and maintain a high level of customer service.

When you first start a home-based gourmet cookie

business, orders are sporadic. You might have none one week and 15 the next. It takes time for sales to become more consistent and good financial planning to make it to the point where they are, but when it comes to building a business around something you love, it's worth it.

Pros and Cons

The best things about starting a gourmet cookie business:

Flexibility to limit the number of orders per week/type of cookies

Marketing a gourmet cookie business is actually pretty fun and relatively simple

There are multiple avenues for growth and/or expansion

The not-so-great things about starting a gourmet cookie business:

The joy you get from baking might start to fade

Planning ahead can be difficult

Eventually, you'll have to invest in baking ware that's specifically for the business

Start-up Costs

If you already have the needed supplies and equipment, your highest start-up cost will be in actually establishing your business. In addition to the establishment costs listed in Chapter Two, you'll also have the costs of marketing, packaging, and ingredients.

When you're first launching, you can keep marketing costs limited to business cards and sticker labels. Prices vary based on multiple factors, such as vendor/shop, quality of design, the durability of the material, and quantity, but you'll need to budget a minimum of $50 for business cards and $60 for labels.

In addition, plan to spend at least $120 on packaging for your first few weeks in business.

Once orders start coming in, ingredients will pay for

themselves; before that, you'll need to foot the bill. The amount you need to budget here depends on the ingredients required for your cookies. When determining how much you need to budget for ingredients, it's better to overestimate.

Budget about $100 for ingredients, initially. In other words, cookies for marketing your business. Then have another $100-$150 in petty cash to cover ingredients for your first dozen or more orders.

Estimated Start-up Cost: $430-$480

Understanding Costs

First, decide what type of cookies you're going to sell. It's best to start with a limited selection. List the ingredients needed for each and the amount of each ingredient for the batch size you're capable of producing.

Next, look up the average market price/per quantity of each ingredient. This will fluctuate, but for now, you just need a solid estimate. Then, times that number by the quantity needed. For instance, if you need two cans of baking powder at $1.89 a can, your total baking soda cost is $3.78.

Once you know the cost of each ingredient in the quantities you need, at the costs of all the ingredients together to determine a soft total. Then, add $25-$30 to that for your estimated ingredient costs at launch.

Determining Price

Determine the cost per serving of ingredients by dividing the overall cost of the ingredient by the number of servings it yields.

Cost / Quantity = Cost Per Serving

Then establish the cost per batch by multiplying the cost per serving by the number of servings used in the recipe.

Cost Per Serving x Number of Servings in One
Batch = Cost of Ingredient Per Batch

Narrow it down even further by dividing that answer by the number of cookies made in a single batch.

Ingredient Cost Per Batch / Number of Cookies Per Batch = Cost Per Cookie

Example: The price for a 25-pound bag of flour is $12. You need four cups of flour to make 48 cookies.

1. 25 / 12 = $2.08 per cup.

2. $2.08 x 4 (number of cups needed per batch) = $8.33 per batch.

3. $8.33 / 48 (number of cookies in batch) = $0.17 per cookie.

The sum of the cost per batch of all ingredients is the soft total cost per batch. Add to that number the cost of man-hours and packaging to get a more accurate total.

Cost of Ingredients Per Batch + Man-Hour Cost Per Batch + Packaging Cost Per Batch = Estimated Cost Per Batch

Add a 20 percent profit margin to the estimated cost per

batch to get an idea of what your prices should look like.

Example:

Ingredient Cost Per Batch = $17.79

Man-Hour Cost Per Batch = $15

Packaging Cost Per Batch = $5.83

The estimated cost per batch before profit margin $38.62, and the total estimated cost per batch is $46.34.

That's $0.96 per cookie if there are 48 cookies in a batch.

With this information in hand and your ideal customer in mind, determine what you should charge per unit and compare those prices to prices of similar cookies at similar businesses in similar areas. If your cookies are significantly less or more expensive than the competitions, consider the reasons why before moving forward.

Systems Check

Prepare to launch with a system check. Make a couple batches of cookies, noting any changes in time, quantity, quality from what you previously estimated.

Set up a packaging station, and after the cookies have cooled, package them like you would if you were selling to a customer. Be sure the package looks presentable and includes your business card.

Once the full batch is packaged, test your cookie delivery method. If you are shipping them in the mail, send a couple boxes to yourself. If you'll be delivering them to individual customers or stores, place the packages in your car and go for a ride. If customers will be picking them up, put them in your designated storage place for pick-ups, then after a few hours, have a friend help you simulate a pick-up transaction.

If any process or product is flawed, now is the time to identify it and deal with it.

How to Sell It

This part will be fun. Start with marketing samples, which in addition to getting the word out about your new business, will likely garner quite a few smiles.

Marketing samples should be limited to one to six cookies, depending on the size and type of cookie. You may need to order special packaging, specifically for a smaller quantity.

In advance of actually handing out your samples, determine the best places to hand them out. Consider nearby businesses and organizations. Coffee shops are a great place both to pass out cookie samples and to vet out the possibility of selling your cookies there. Unless otherwise permitted, avoid schools, hospitals, retail shops, restaurants, and other bakeries.

On hand-out day, make sure your sample packages look pretty, and each one has a business card attached. When you arrive at a handout location, introduce yourself and request permission to leave a few samples or pass them out yourself.

It may help to memorize a short script in advance.
Something simple. Like:

> "Hi, I'm Sue Ann. I recently started a cookie
> delivery business, and I just wanted to bring you a
> free sample of my coconut truffles and lemon drops.
> If you have any questions about
> ingredients/allergens, all the nutritional
> information is on my website."

In addition to in-person marketing, take to Facebook to
promote your new business and ask friends to like and
share your posts.

Estimated Earnings

Once you get your gourmet cookie company off the
ground, you can expect to earn anywhere from $400-$800
a week if you're working 20 hours or more per week.
However, if you expand to include catering services or
other gourmet treats or land a few recurring orders, you
can make as much as $1,200 per week.

Gourmet Dog Biscuits

Business Description

With a gourmet dog biscuit business, much of your time will be spent baking and packaging dog treats, but as with all home businesses, a fair amount of time will also have to go to attract customers.

In addition to staying atop customers' minds, depending on where you live, you may be competing for customers with one or more brick-and-mortar dog bakeries, which means you have to come up with an angle that makes your business stand out.

Whatever that something is — delivery services, organic treats, wholesales, subscription boxes, etc. — you'll need to allot a portion of your time to developing, perfecting, and marketing it.

The good news is many pet bakeries start in people's kitchens and end up on the shelves of national chain stores.

Pros and Cons

The best things about starting a gourmet dog biscuits business:

> You can sell online and run your business completely from home

> The option of wholesale or selling direct to customer

> The stats for success bode well

> There's franchise potential

> Few requirements for selling at farmer's markets, community events

The less-than-ideal things about starting a gourmet dog biscuits business:

> The market for gourmet dog biscuits isn't universal — location matters

Damage liability if regulations aren't followed, and dogs are harmed

Investment in separate baking supplies

Start-up Costs

Aside from establishment costs and baking supplies, you'll need to budget for marketing, packaging, ingredients, and distribution.

For now, to keep costs low, you can market your business for free on social media, with print materials, like business cards, flyers, and sticker labels; and through word of mouth.

Plan to spend about $120 on business cards, flyers, and sticker labels, $75 for packaging materials, and another $100 for ingredients. Finally, you'll want to have $175 in petty cash to cover marketing opportunities, materials for meetings with stores and pet shop managers, and other costs that may arise during your rollout.

Distribution costs are hard to estimate without a specific

business model but plan to at least have enough set-aside to cover transportation or the shipment of a dozen or so samples.

Total Start-up Costs: $400

Understanding Costs

To determine the cost, start by making a list the includes each ingredient and the amount needed per batch for each of the types of dog biscuits you plan to offer at launch.

Next, look up and note the size and average market rate of each ingredient. Determine the cost per ingredient by dividing the quantity or size sold by the price. For instance, a five-pound bag of carobs that sells for $15 is $3 per pound. There are about two cups of carob chips in a pound, so you can pretty accurately estimate the carob cost per batch of that particular biscuit at $3.

When you've determined the cost of each ingredient, add them all together for the overall cost of ingredients per batch. Add to that the cost of packaging. Next, add in the cost in man-hours. The sum is a pretty good estimate of your total cost per batch.

For example, if it takes you 45 minutes to bake and package one batch and your hourly rate is $15, the man-hour cost is $11.25. Add that to the cost of ingredients and packaging — say $19.91 — to get to an estimated total cost of $31.16 per batch. If one batch yields 48 biscuits, the cost per biscuit is about 65 cents.

Knowing your costs is not only essential to budgeting and long-term planning, but it also helps determine your prices.

Determining Prices

Add a 20 percent profit margin to the cost of each batch. This new total should be your starting point when you decide the price of your biscuits.

Using the example above, the total cost per batch with a 20 percent profit margin baked is about $37.40. We'll round it up to $38 for ease. You may also want to tack on an extra $2 to cover the cost of gas, electricity, water, and dish soap required to bake, clean, and package.

The lowest these biscuits should be priced at is about $10 per dozen or 83 cents individually. Now, consider your target market. What are the demographics like?

If your niche serves the affluent, it might make sense to hike those prices — perhaps considerably. If your target market is college students and young graduates, keeping prices low will attract more customers.

Finally, bear in mind, the price per unit usually drops as quantity increases. So, in this scenario, you may want to price individual biscuits at $1.50 each, four-packs at $5.00, and a box of a dozen at $12.

Systems Check

Before taking your biscuits to market, see how well they're received by canine customers. Your dogs may love them, but that doesn't mean all dogs will. If you get a couple dozen or more positive reactions, you can take them to market with confidence, and it has the added perk of providing an opportunity to get images, quotes, and ratings to use on marketing materials.

How to Sell It

Dog biscuits can be sold directly to the consumer or to third-party retailers and businesses. The benefit of the latter is higher profit margins, larger contract sizes, and the ability to plan ahead. But getting your biscuits in the local pet shop or grocery store will require a bit of work.

If you know a small business owner, grocery manager, or buyer for a chain store, use your connections. Once your established and have sales data from one retailer, other retailers will be more open to selling your biscuits

Without connections, getting in stores will likely require having a solid customer base, being able to provide enticing sales data points, and knowing how to market your product. Networking with other business owners through your local chamber of commerce is helpful too.

To develop a customer base, consider a summer debut at a farmer's market, social media marketing, and seeing if you can handout or drop off free samples at nearby doggy day cares, pet-friendly cafes, grooming salons, and dog-related meet-up groups.

Come up with a fun social media promotion to get your name out there. Keep it simple or get creative with it — as long as it gets people talking about your business, it's a good thing. Ideally, the promotion should result in people posting on your page or sharing a post from you.

For example, the cutest dog contest where people post pictures on your page and vote (via likes) for their favorite. Or submit captions or fill-in a thought bubble on pictures you post. Collect entries, then on the pre-determined day, post them and ask the public to vote on the funniest. The dog or caption with the most votes wins a month's supply of biscuits.

Make a habit of carrying fresh treat samples and business cards with you when you're out and about. You never know when an opportunity to build relationships will arise.

Whether you're walking in the park and stop to say hi to a friendly, four-legged fur ball or if the person cutting your hair will mention the mastiff waiting at home for them. When the timing is right, make sure you have everything you need to showcase your business.

Estimated Earnings

The internet is chock full of tales of wildly successful pet bakeries, and pet treats companies, and investors dropping hundreds of thousands on dog treats that fulfill a specific niche.

Meal Prep Service

Business Description

It seems people are busier than ever, and for many of us, one of the first things to go when life gets hectic is quality home-cooked meals. Are you the one that can solve this problem in your local community?

There are different ways you can set-up a meal prep business, but all require cooking experience, creativity, and organization skills. We'll discuss a few approaches here.

There's private, in-home meal preparation, where you would travel to private residences, prep two to four dinners, package them in provided containers and label each with heating instructions.

The best part of this option is the low, up-front cost. While arrangements on how groceries are acquired and who picks out the recipes may vary, the clients are responsible for the cost, and you use their kitchenware and equipment

The costs are a little higher for pre-order and day-of-meal prep businesses, as you'll need to cover the cost of ingredients, equipment, and supplies up-front.

Planning is easier for pre-order meal prep businesses because customers select the meals, quantity, and timing or orders in advance, allowing you to determine timelines and ingredient quantities up-front.

However, the downside to this set-up is the competition, both real and perceived. Many meal delivery subscription services come ready-to-prepare, not ready-to-heat — to succeed with customers, you'll need to market the difference.

Day-of meal prep could be a hot commodity in many areas — (semi) last-minute fresh, home-cooked meals. With this type of business, you'll offer one to three options a day and take orders up-until a certain time for ready-to-heat meal delivery by a certain time that evening.

This takes careful planning, a keen awareness of food prices, last-minute and often fast-paced purchasing and preparing, the ability to quickly substitute ingredients without affecting the outcome, and a bit of good luck.

Having a couple of business partners or friends willing to work for leftovers would also be helpful. Without a few helping hands, you may have to place a low cap on the number of orders accepted each day.

Pros and Cons

Pros:

You can meal prep for yourself at the same time

Ready-to-heat meal prep has limited competition

Ability to franchise if successful

Easy marketing with strategically placed flyers

Lunch-only service potential in business districts

Cons

Identifying and catering to a specific target market
is critical to success

A good website is a must

Food safety certifications required

Coordinating delivery times and schedules

May require working with third party delivery
service

Market Segments and Potential

Use the resources here, social media, local demographic
sources, and your own keen insights, determine what
market segments are available to you, and decide which

one you'll service.

Working Families

Diabetic Diet

Heart-Conscious Diet

Gluten-Free

Senior Citizens

Dairy-Free

Keto Diet

Vegetarian

Vegan

Low-Sodium

College Students

It's best to limit your focus to just one market segment when launching; however, you may find a cross-over between two or more segments that fit with a single marketing strategy.

Research local demographics to determine what markets are most robust in your area. The U.S. Census Bureau website is a great place to start. The Bureau of Labor Statistics and the Center for Disease Control websites are also great research tools.

Licenses, Permits, and Certifications

License, permit, and certification requirements vary by state, and you'll need to check with your state business offices, city hall, and local health department to get the full picture of what's required for you to start a meal-prep business at home.

Note: In-home meal prep may be considered domestic work, forgoing the need for licenses, permits, and certifications.

You'll likely need to get a Safe Food Handling Certification and a Food Manager's Certificate, both of which can be obtained online through SERV Safe. Costs vary by state and can range from as little as $15 to as much as $30.

Start-up Costs

After establishment, licensing, and certification, status costs for meal prep businesses aren't exuberant.

If you're doing private, in-home service, the only thing you have to budget for is marketing and transportation to clients. To get started, budget at least $75 marketing and another $50 for petty cash/transportation.

Private, In-Home Meal Prep: $125

For pre-order meal prep, your budget should include marketing, packaging, delivery, and petty cash. Plan to spend about $150 on marketing — for business cards, flyers, social media ads, and more — $150 on packaging for the first couple weeks and have a minimum of $200 in petty cash.

Depending on the methods of payment accepted and the accuracy of your pricing, the benefit of having customers order and pay in advance is not having to cover the cost of ingredients up front. The cost of delivery is affected by various factors. You'll need to research your options. Make sure the cost of delivery is reflected in your pricing or check-out options.

Pre-Order Meal Prep: $500

Day-of meal prep comes with the same costs as pre-order, but it's a good idea to up the marketing budget and, because of payment processing times, you'll also need to budget for ingredients. Plan to have a minimum of $200 for marketing, $100 for packaging, $250 for ingredients, and $200 in petty cash.

Day-of Meal Prep: $750

Determining Price

In the restaurant industry, the rule of thumb is that your food costs should not exceed 30 percent of the menu price for that item. That means if something costs $5 to prepare, it should be priced at no less than $17.

Pricing for meal prep services isn't the same, but the idea is similar. Your prices should include the cost of ingredients, packaging, man-hours, delivery, and profit while remaining affordable to your target market.

If your ready-to-heat lasagna yields 32 servings at the cost of $15, it costs 47 cents per serving. Add in man-hours next — let's say $20 — and packaging — let's do $1.10 per individual serving — and your new total is $70.80 or $2.25 per serving. Next, add a 25 percent profit margin.

The total cost is now $88.50 for 32 servings, but the price of ingredients wavers over time. Yours should. Play it safe by adding in $1.50 of wiggle room per serving. Let's say delivery is $3.

The absolute minimum you can charge per serving of lasagna is $7.27.

Does that price fit the budget and spending habits of your target market? If not, increasing the price or decrease expenses to lower the cost.

How to Sell It

Your marketing strategy will depend largely on the demographics and characteristics of your target audience. Distributing flyers has proven beneficial to many meal prep businesses. Grocery stores and building lobbies are great places to hang flyers.

Places to advertise via flyers:

Gyms

Health/Medical Centers

Senior Centers

Health Food Stores

Community Centers

Office Buildings

Residential Buildings

Nearby Schools

Athletic Shops

The best places for you to post flyers will be unique to your niche. If you're servicing the elderly, consider posting flyers at your local recreation or senior activities center.

Remember to get permission before you post and consider offering coupons and/or discounts when needed. For example, you may need to offer a discount to parents, staff, and teachers; or offer a giveback, such as 50 percent of all profits on all "name of school" orders will be donated to the school.

Once your distribution area is well-papered, focus your marketing efforts online. Announce the opening of your business on social media and consider rolling out a short-term marketing campaign from an official business page.

Also consider, providing a meal prep demonstration at your local library or civic center, partnering with a local charity for a fundraising drive, or donating a week's worth of meals to a charity auction.

Estimated Earnings

Successful meal prep start-ups have monthly profits in the range of five to seven percent. That means that as the owner of a meal prep start-up that does about $37,000 in sales monthly, you'll be making about $2,200 per month. It might not put you on the fast track to being a millionaire, but as you grow, expand your service area and take on staff, the percentage of profit you make will steadily tick upwards.

Chapter Six: Jobs for the Animal Lover

Whether you just like going on walks and don't mind picking up poo or you're just naturally good with animals of all kinds, if you enjoy spending time with fur balls, starting a pet-centric business just might leave you howling with delight. This section takes a closer look at two animal-centric start-ups: dog walking and pet training services.

Working with animals can be a deeply rewarding and enriching experience — one that many people say doesn't feel like work at all — but as is the rule in life, it has its challenges. Your success in this field is dependent on your ability to react quickly, calmly, and deliberately to those challenges.

Pros and Cons

Pros:

Choice of Work Settings — home, client home, outdoors

Emotionally Rewarding

Current and Projected Industry Growth

Non-Sedentary

Schedule Flexibility

Cons:

Dangerous if Ill-Equipped

Dual Liability — Damage to or Caused by Animal in Your Care

Physically Demanding

Risk of Injury

Cleaning Up Feces and Urine

Getting Started

Step One: Research licensing and certification. There are currently no licensing requirements for the type of non-medical, animal-related work suggested here; however, some municipalities require permits for animal care work. To ensure your start-up is on the right side of the law, take a little time to research the law in your city and county.

While you're at it, it's worth looking into certifications — find out who offers them, what it costs, how to get one, and the benefits or disadvantages of having or not having one. (See specific sections for more information.)

Step Two: Come up with a name for your business and check to see if it is available.

Step Three: Make it official. Determine how you want to structure your business, file the forms needed, register a domain name and make it official.

Step Four: Apply for city/county required permits and licenses.

Step Five: Collect and build media. If possible, get a few pictures of you actually working with animals or of your canine customers. They don't need to be professional quality, just good enough to look sharp on a website or in marketing materials. You can certainly use stock photos but use them sparingly. And, when it comes to taking your own photos, remember — more is better. Snap as many as possible. You can narrow them down later.

Step Six: Create a logo.

Step Seven: Determine your costs and prices.

Step Eight: Build a website.

Step Nine: Order print materials and packaging. Buy Ingredients. (See Specific Start-up Types)

Step Ten: Do a test run. (See Specific Start-up Types)

Dog Walking Business

Business Description

This job will provide you with plenty of fresh air, exercise, and furry fans, but it's not for everyone. For this business to be successful, you'll need to be organized, on time, communicative and responsive. You also have to like dogs. If you check all those boxes, this is a start-up worth considering.

Starting a dog walking business is low-cost, and most places' requirements are scant. However, just because certain things — like insurance and certification aren't required — doesn't mean they aren't worth considering.

Multiple providers offer insurance specific to dog walkers, which covers you should a dog in your care get hurt, hurt someone else, or damage property. It's not too pricey either. Most policies have an annual cost of between $150-$300.

It may also behoove you to become certified in animal first aid and CPR. You can do it online in under an hour and for less than $100 (there are classes as cheap as $40). Not only is pet first aid certification a great selling point, but it will help you know what to do in an emergency situation.

Finally, to prevent emergency situations and injuries to yourself, others, and the dogs in your care educate yourself on signs of fear and aggression in dogs.

Pros and Cons

Pros

   You get to be around dogs all day

   No office drama

Independence and flexibility

Healthy lifestyle

Cons

Dogs still need walking in the rain and snow

Takes time to build a steady client base

Working with and relying on difficult human (or dog) clients

Start-up Costs

This is one low-cost start-up. After establishment, your costs are limited to marketing, transportation, and personal gear and supplies.

Budget $145 for marketing, $30 for transportation, $100 for personal gear and supplies, and $25 for petty cash. Whatever you don't spend should be added to petty cash or reinvested into the business elsewhere.

Of your marketing budget, you should earmark about $50 for professional business cards. The remaining $95 can be used on flyers, magnets, treat bags with your card attached, social media ads, or whatever else will garner the attention of your target audience.

Your personal gear and supplies budget should go towards poo bags, an extra leash, collapsible water bowl, reusable water bottle, and whatever gear you may need to accept your first few clients. That may include walking shoes, socks, a ball cap, rain boots, gloves, or sunscreen.

Determining Prices

Your upfront costs are so low, they don't have a significant factor in how you price your services, instead dog walking businesses usually charge by blocks of time in 15-, 20-, 30- or 45-minute increments, as well as the number of dogs.

Most walkers charge between $15-$20 for 20-minute walks and $20-$30 for 30-minute walks for the first dog. Each additional dog after that adds another $5-$10 to the price.

However, your rates per time-block shouldn't be the only way you charge. If a client has two dogs, you shouldn't charge the same rate for the second dog. Instead, charge a flat-rate fee of $5-$10 for each additional dog.

And it pays to offer discounts for multiple visits in a single service day, on-going contracts, multiple walk packages, and building or group bookings. For example, if five or more tenants in the same building coordinate service times/days, it qualifies them for a discounted rate. The idea is to incentives arrangements that benefit your business and make it easier for you to run it on a day-to-day basis.

Tips for Success

Always obtain a signed contract.

Contracts should spell out what's included in the service, how much it costs, and when payment is due.

Research successful dog walking businesses in similar areas and adopt a similar approach to yours.

Educate yourself on dog behavior, breeds, first aid, and handling.

Set policies, limitations, availability, and stick to them.

Maintain detailed records of each human and dog client. The record should include the client name, address and contact info, emergency contacts and the dog's name, date of birth, breed, color, veterinarian, vaccination record, and other pertinent health and behavioral information.

How to Sell It

There's plenty of low-cost, high-return marketing opportunities for dog walkers, but determining just which ones are right for you and your burgeoning business requires knowing where and how to reach your target market.

When it comes to marketing a dog walking business, don't underestimate the power of paper. Or, to be more specific, business cards and flyers.

Get in the habit of carrying your business cards with you

every time you leave the house and make an effort to engage in friendly small talk. This might not be the most proactive measure, but you'll be surprised by how often it proves serendipitous.

Next, make eye-catching or clever flyers and strategically post them around town at pet stores, dog parks, community centers, grocery stores, veterinary clinics, public transportation hubs, apartment building lobbies, restaurants that get business lunch rushes, and anywhere else that your target clientele may frequent.

This may seem to go against a competitive instinct, but networking with other dog walkers —as well as pet sitters, boarding facilities, and pet salons — can pay off big time. Fellow dog walkers are apt to refer clients outside their service area or pass along your name to interested customers when their roster is too full to take on new clients.

Promote your business online through social media, a well-designed website, and a presence on listing sites like Yelp.

Get creative with unique ways to help your dog walking business standout from the pack. Maybe personalized webcam links where pet parents can log on during walk times and see what their fur baby is seeing from a mini cam that you attach to collars during walks. Or, personal portholes, clients can log into to see your route, updates, and an occasional picture.

Finally, consider social media contests, bark cards, chew toys or poo bags with your logo, and any other promo to which your target audience is likely to respond.

Estimated Earnings

The average monthly salary for dog walkers in the U.S. is about $2,500. Not bad for a job that gets you outdoors, exercising, and hanging out with fur balls, but as the owner of a dog walking business, that's just the starting point. Sure, you have more expenses than an independent dog walker, but with those expenses comes the ability to earn revenue without doing the work. For example, if you hire a part-time employee at a rate of $15 an hour who works 10 hours a week doing 18 25-minute walks that are priced at $25 each, you'll make a profit of about $280 weekly.

Dog Training Services

Business Description

You don't have to go to school, take classes, do an apprenticeship, or get certified for this start-up, but you do have to have plenty of knowledge on and experience with pets, in particular dogs.

Pet trainers work with pets and their people towards a variety of ends, but most commonly, it is to address bad behavior and/or instill obedience. Other more specialized types of training include search and rescue, therapy, cadaver search, law enforcement, hunting, entertainment, protection, detection, sports, and working with livestock.

For people who get more excited to see the dog than the person walking it, being a dog trainer probably seems like a dream come true. However, this isn't necessarily the case. Sure, dog trainers teach dogs behaviors and commands, but they also have to teach their human parents how to make commands, respond to behavior good and bad, and recognize the signs of fear, anxiety, and aggression in Fido.

When it comes down to it, trainers spend half their time training the dog and the other half training the human. In order for your pet training services business to be successful, you need to be good with both species.

Common Methods of Training:

Koehler Method

Clicker Training

Dominance-Based Training

Negative Reinforcement

Relationship-Based Training

While these methods vary in form, they share key aspects, such as knowing the animal's personality and attributes, acute timing of reinforcement or punishment, and consistent communication.

However, the most successful trainers have also developed methods for getting their human clients to stick with what they learned during training once training is complete. In other words, in order for your dog training start-up to become successful, you need to like people, be patient and be able to employ different training styles based on the personalities and lifestyles of pet parents.

Pros and Cons

Pros

Various options for specialization

You won't be office-bound or sedentary

Trainers report feeling emotionally fulfilled and satisfied with their careers

Ability to schedule sessions inside or outside

Cons

Requires working with pets and pet parents

Physically demanding

Can be dangerous at times

Start-up Costs

Since licensing isn't require, the establishment costs for a pet training business are pretty low. However, you'll also need to budget for insurance, software, supplies, and marketing.

Insurance for dog trainers starts at about $220 per year, but the average cost in the U.S. is $250-$700 per year.

Insurance Estimate: $230

A variety of software programs specifically for dog training businesses is available on the market. Each has its own benefits, drawbacks, and unique attributes, but most of the programs out there include all or most of the following features: availability calendar, booking tool, payment tool, vaccine records, progress tracker; report cards, accounting reports, text messaging and pet profiles.

Some programs also feature email marketing, client profiles, client dashboards, document storage, QuickBooks integration, payroll, time clocks, form templates, lesson plans, attendance records, and other features designed to help you run a dog training business.

The price of these programs varies almost as much as their features. The majority of programs are between $30-$60 per month; however, there are some for as little as $20 per month and a few that are upwards of $100 a month.

Three-Month Software Estimate: $100

You could spend a fortune on supplies, but when you're first starting out, it's a good idea to keep your purchases limited to essential supplies only. You should budget for leashes, harnesses, clickers, treats, disinfectant spray, pee pads, muzzles, portable mats, target sticks, collars, and barriers.

You don't have to buy in bulk just yet, but you'll need to

have enough in stock to cover use by both you and each client present during training, as well as replacements should an item get damaged during a session.

Initial Supplies Estimate: $150

Finally, you should set at least a little something aside to use for marketing purposes. You don't have to spend a lot on marketing right out of the gate, but you can't duck out of this expense entirely. You'll definitely need business cards, and you may want to consider brochures, flyers, promotional gear, and paid social media advertisements.

Initial Marketing Cost Estimate: $75

Estimated Three-Month Start-up Cost: $555

How to Sell It

Getting out there and meeting fellow professionals in the industry is invaluable to growing your business as a dog trainer. Make a point of introducing yourself to and attending animal/pet-industry networking and trade show events.

Reach out to veterinary clinics, breeders, shelters, pet supply stores, groomers, boarding facilities, and dog walkers and try to strike mutually beneficial recommendation deals, where they refer clients to you, and you refer clients to them. Request permission to leave a few cards and/or brochures in the reception area of any brick-and-mortar businesses.

If they have a website that features resources and services for pet parents, see if they'll list you there. However, you'll likely need to do the same and include them in a listing of resources and services on your website.

Consider flyers, too. Try to get permission to hang them up in or near dog parks and anywhere else pet parents frequent. Get your name out there online with a quality website, one or two social media business pages, and on listing sites like Yelp.

Finally, show off your skills. Bring your dog to a public place and put on a performance. Make a habit of returning to the same park at the same time every Sunday afternoon, so interested on-lookers know how to locate you when they tell others about you or need your services themselves.

Then, pick one or two days a week to display your skills at other public places and events. You don't have to do it forever, but until you have a full roster of clients, it will pay off to show off.

Finally, when you're able to allocate a bit more towards marketing, consider investing in some promotional gear. You can put your logo on just about anything these days. Imagine what yours would look like on clickers, poo bag dispensers, throwing balls, squeaky toys, or a bag of treats.

Estimated Earnings

The estimated earnings for dog trainers vary by location and specialization. On the low end of the salary spectrum, obedience trainers earn an average of $36,000 a year. On the high end, they're making an average of $53,000-$55,000, although, in places like Southern California, it's not uncommon to see obedience trainers who earn upwards of $60,000 annually.

Service trainers earn an average of $17,000 — that's specifically from training service dogs — many supplement their base income by teaching training classes part-time, for which they charge anywhere from $20-$50 per hour. A specialization in training therapy dogs brings in an average of $29,000 per year.

Trainers who specialize in training detection dogs or search and rescue dogs earn from $47,000 to $98,000 annually in America (that includes detection of drugs, cadaver, and explosives), with explosives detection situated comfortably near the top of the range. Entertainment or movie animal trainers earn between $25,000 and $55,000 per year.

The majority of trainers who specialize in training protection dogs and/or guard dogs report earnings of about $35,000-$37,000 per year, with an overall salary range of $31,500 to $59,000.

In short, a dog training start-up can expect to earn as little as $17,000 or as much as $98,000 annually, depending on where they are located, what they specialize in, who their clientele is, how good they are at what they do, and how well they market it.

Chapter Seven: Jobs for the Number Ninja

What's the number ninja all about? Are you good at
crunching numbers or working with balance sheets? Then
running a bookkeeping and accounting services business
is a call in the right direction.

Presumably, you've been an accountant or bookkeeper at
a private firm some years back and are willing to set up
your own business. Or chances are that you can't seem to
find an open position. It's time to get off the couch and get

busy with your fingers and mind.

In truth, business owners, entrepreneurs, and other entities will always need one service or another. No man is an island. Not all of them are good with numbers or organization. They need someone to run the operations behind the scenes, one who can point their finances in the right direction. With this in mind, you can utilize your skills in meeting their goals.

Running a bookkeeping or accounting practice provides self-accomplishment. It gives you that feeling of meeting a need. And in this case, there are several demands in this area.

Business Description

People tend to interchange "Accounting" and "Bookkeeping." But here is the thing; they are two entirely different occupations. So, what makes them different? Bookkeeping involves the monitoring of the inflow and outflow of money in a business. The bookkeeper ensures that there are accurate financial records to monitor monetary activities.

Bookkeepers are backed by the International Association of Bookkeepers (IAB). This is the world's largest bookkeeping institution. What roles do these professionals perform? They provide small-scale and medium-sized businesses and enterprises with the following:

Inventory of daily cash flow within the business.

Analysis of VAT returns and year-end tax planning strategies.

Efficient operation of finances.

Pros and Cons

Pros

You can start and operate a bookkeeping business with less cost.

Promoting business marketability has never been this easy. It is possible to gain experience in one accounting application, becoming a specialist in the process.

Bookkeeping does not require formal training or certifications. Nevertheless, it is a plus to become certified.

It provides you with the opportunity to work remotely, regardless of your location. All you need is a target market.

Cons

Tendencies of incurring liability problems are present in this business.

Client privacy is of utmost priority. Failure to do so comes with dire consequences.

It may require keeping abreast of technological gadgets to oversee clients' businesses.

Purchasing and updating bookkeeping tools, including software, can be financially draining.

Start-up Costs

You can run a bookkeeping services business with less than $500 as it dwells more on gaining relevant industry knowledge. Interestingly, it is easy to access bookkeeping courses online. The following organizations provide qualifications in this field as well:

Chartered Institute of Management Accountants (CIMA)

Association of Accounting Technicians (AAT)

Association of Chartered Certified Accountants (ACCA)

International Associations of Bookkeepers (IAB)

Institute of Chartered Accountants in England and Wales (ICAEW)

Association of Accounting Technicians (AAT)

Some of these organizations, such as IAB, provide would-be bookkeepers with courses backed by QiW (Qualifications in Wales), Ofqual (The Office of Qualifications and Examinations Regulation), and CCEA (Council for the Curriculum, Examinations & Assessment).

Qualifications are of three categories:

Award in Bookkeeping

Award in Computerized Bookkeeping

Award in Computerized Accounting for Business

As stated before, it is not mandatory to become a certified public bookkeeper. However, considering the world, we live in today where certification and expertise rule, you can't overlook the place of training.

You can undertake bookkeeping courses and certification programs in community colleges. Interestingly, some of them provide other services, including loan packaging, tax preparation, and software training. QuickBooks is an ideal example. In the same vein, the American Institute of Professional Bookkeepers provides such certifications.

How to Sell It

Having received the right training, it is time to launch your bookkeeping business. However, one element comes to play at this point – setting the ideal rate. In determining the amount to charge, you have to consider the following:

Your target audience niche

Your target audience needs

Your bookkeeping experiences

Services provided

Your client's business size

Most bookkeepers charge by the hour or month. Some even request a retainer fee for their services. Typically, in

Europe, these professionals charge £25 per hour, depending on the job type. You can provide your client with a fixed fee to give them a total idea of what to expect financially.

Setting bookkeeping fees does not involve waving a magic wand. You have to find the right balance between charging too high and charging too low.

Nevertheless, you should not underrate your value, including the vast training and certification received from reputable organizations. In analyzing your next step on commencing your bookkeeping business, you need to come up with a business plan:

Find out who your clients are. Do you intend to work with micro-enterprises or businesses (less than 10 employees), small-scale businesses (maximum of 50 employees), or sole proprietors?

How will you source your target audience? Perhaps, you may choose to consider freelance sites, local advertising, your previous place of employment, family and friends, word of mouth, or even website and social media advertising.

Determine the service you intend to offer. This is not limited to payroll management, bank deposits, cash receipts documentation, annual budget maintenance, and supplier invoice payments. Before doing this, find out the needs of your target audience. What are they looking for?

Choose your work mode with your clients. Will it be a contract-based or one-off bookkeeping service?

It is worth noting that these factors are integral parts of one's bookkeeping business plan. Another aspect to consider is the duration of such a plan? Are you considering a year, two years, five years, or even seven years? Think in the direction of:

Business turnover

Business expansion

Staff employment

Do not overlook the place of business research and planning when starting your bookkeeping services. This will help you to define your path and achieve your goals.

So, what happens after your exams and qualifications? It is time to enroll in the Institute of Certified Bookkeepers (ICB) or any other regulated organization listed above. Apply for a practice license.

It is essential not to forget the anti-money laundering rules and code of professional conduct. Why is that important?

In truth, you have to help your client reduce the risk of money laundering by providing legal support. Without understanding and adhering to the money laundering rules, you can't be of service to these individuals.

The Code of Professional Conduct encapsulates the fundamental principles of ethics and professional conduct. This is your responsibility to the ICB. Violation of such terms may incur disciplinary action. Insurance is another element to include in setting up a bookkeeping service, the reason being that clients have business needs.

And guess what? Mistakes are bound to occur. How do you protect your clients against such? Insurance is their haven. With such, they stay happy. How important is this insurance? It keeps your financial interests safe, limiting business disruptions and covering the cost of fixing business errors. For example, it caters to your business needs even when a client refuses to pay you.

Public liability insurance protects you from claims from third parties for personal injury and property damage.

Once these factors are in place, it is time to start the bookkeeping business. Kindly remember; it is important to register with the HMRC as a self-employed entity. The exception to this is if you have a limited company.

Does your work entail the use of an office space? Or do you prefer working from home? Setting up an office space is no walk in the park. However, there are coworking spaces available to help you cut down costs. This is a better opportunity compared to renting a personal office apartment.

If this is your first time running a business, do not shirk

your day's work. One of the merits attached to this business is the ability to source clients that you can serve after working hours. They may come from contacts made during your current job.

As time progresses, your client-base will expand, creating several business decisions along the way. One of them may include asking this question – Should I quit my job and spend my entire time running the bookkeeping business or just run it part-time?

It is not uncommon to find bookkeepers working from home. Clients may be sourced from their homes, offices, local coffee shops, and other places. But it is recommended to rent small office space as soon as the business commences.

The reason for such a move hinges on the fact that clients are entrusting their money into your care. Working from home may not bear a professional look. You need a formal working environment to convey the right message. Remember your privacy and your clients' confidentiality is needed to ensure smooth business operations.

If you have people living with you – family members or friends – clients may view such an environment as being unsafe for business transactions. Lastly, organizing business meetings in your residential space can cause inconvenience to your clients.

Look for a company that offers office space for rent instead of a traditional lease. There are similar places in big cities.

Ask friends who own businesses if there is extra space to rent and if that fails, look for traditional office space. Single office rent is not as strange as you might think.

What if you decide to work from home? In that case, designate a section of your home to your work. This can be a spare room or a portion of your living room. Have a place to store all paperwork. Purchasing power is an essential element as well.

How much can you set aside for a PC? What accounting software and business stationery will you need? There is also the need to create a business bank account. These are factors you can't ignore.

In managing the bookkeeping business processes, the use of digital software becomes paramount. Such systems help to monitor business activities in real-time. With the results generated, it is possible to report analysis for ideal financial decision-making on behalf of clients.

Having accounting software up and ready isn't limited to accountants. Even as a bookkeeper, you can install and operate this system to provide clients with real-time financial analysis and generate financial statements. There are cloud numbering solutions that help you to access numbers remotely at any time.

As such, it becomes easy to work with clients in real-time, addressing their various bookkeeping needs and answering possible questions.

As a reminder, bookkeeping services can be financially rewarding. Clients can access services needed to sustain and expand their businesses. Number ninjas are always in demand, especially when such individuals are good at organizing financial information. If you fall into this category, then this business idea is right for you.

It is worth noting that state laws request the establishment of an official business structure. One foremost business structure for small-scale enterprises is a limited liability company (LLC).

In several states in the U.S., setting up this entity is straightforward, with costs ranging below the $100 benchmark. More details on this are available on the Secretary of State's online platform. At the same time, you can avail yourself of business registration services. Remember the place of insurance, especially Errors and Exceptions Insurance. Generally, bookkeepers procure this insurance coverage. Another option is general liability.

For cheaper insurance policies, it is recommended that you opt for E&O insurance. You can get some of these coverages for $25 per month.

How about sourcing clients? In truth, they will not come to you at the beginning. You have to find them. As such, having marketing tools and materials is one of the keys to building a client-base. If you are aesthetically inclined, you can design the materials yourself.

Otherwise, several templates and freelance designers are out there to help you with your project. Also, their prices are affordable.

Find out from other professional bookkeepers in the industry what clients need. Check out marketing materials from other bookkeeping companies. Are they intricate and stressful? Why is this important? These professional organizations have paved the way in terms of market research and competitive analysis. They have the experience of working with clients. Understanding their business process will help you to run yours efficiently.

Having a website improves professionalism and business visibility. Do you want your bookkeeping services to transcend your location? Are you keen on people discovering your offering from anywhere in the world? Then you need a professional website. It should be simple and user-friendly. Include essential information relevant to clients – no fluff.

Traditional marketing can't be ignored. Go through your contact list. Who can you reach out to effectively? Do you need door-to-door marketing? Can you find clients in business functions and community events?

To begin with, reach out to those you know. They could be previous or current colleagues. This is the price you have to pay to set up a promising bookkeeping business.

As soon as you are established, your clients will come around without you making a move. Commencing with customer service will set your business apart from the rest. What additional services can you provide? Are you available after work hours?

How can you cater to clients with needs that are outside your professionalism? Do you have other trusted professionals that can handle such needs? These are some of the questions worth asking.

Do you remember your clients on their birthdays or other special events? This determines how much loyalty you build with your clients.

These individuals are not just "clients"; they are humans with emotions, thoughts, and needs as well. Taking their well-being into consideration is one step to building a reputable bookkeeping business. It is no news that clients complain about the absence of personal and human touch in businesses. Bridging this gap will set you apart.

Estimated Earnings

Not every business owner or entrepreneur is organized — some have a hard time monitoring the financial aspect of their businesses or enterprises. Bookkeeping requires time, dedication, financial knowledge, and the right personality.

In truth, there are smart business gurus out there with disorganized offices. Most of them have minimal time to get their documents in place. Hence, they need someone who can ensure a well-structured working environment.

It may include arranging a stack of bills or bank statements according to respective dates of transactions or even creating an automated system that ensures precise storage of confidential documents.

So, how much do bookkeepers earn? Here is what the Bureau of Labor Statistics has to state. According to studies, Bookkeepers earned a median salary of $35,170 in 2012. In other words, their average earnings by the hour stood at $16.91.

But that is not all there is to this report. There is a projection of additional 204,000 positions in 2022. Such an average rate of growth is nothing short of commendable when weighed against other occupations.

Surprisingly, the statistics represent individuals who oversee the affairs of a single company.

On the other hand, independent professionals in this career path can hit hourly earnings, ranging from $25 to $40. This depends on their work location and the type of job they do.

Working as a bookkeeper over time gives you the platform to gain a strong foothold in this sector, increasing your earnings and client-base. Some of these individuals resort to hiring small staff or more partners as their services expand.

The journey to overseeing hundreds of businesses doesn't

come overnight. A bookkeeper must remain consistent in building a solid client base. This action promotes business visibility and sustainability. Gaining extensive training in this field boost credibility.

If you've had past working experience in overseeing the financial affairs of businesses, then this business is the holy grail you need to become financially independent.

Chapter Eight: Jobs for the Tech Savant

Business Description

What does this term mean? Tech savants are tech-savvy. In other words, they love and spend most of their time on computers and other technological systems. For such individuals, running a computer-based home business is a call in the right direction. Interestingly, people with this interest can conduct their businesses from anywhere in the world, provided they have a PC or smartphone and internet access.

But that is not all. Such individuals must be knowledgeable and skillful in providing satisfactory tech-related services to clients. Starting this business is straightforward and affordable.

Pros and Cons

Pros

You can provide your client with safety and security, increasing demand and profit.

Fewer business expenses. You have no employee to pay salaries – no health care insurance, remunerations, and the rest.

Opportunity to provide 24/7 tech services, maintaining relevance and promoting business visibility.

Provision of optimum customer satisfaction.

Enough time to expand your business.

Cons

Technological knowledge and skills are not sufficient to build a sustainable tech-savvy business. You need good communication skills, marketing skills, and customer relationship management (CRM).

Marketing such services can be expensive.

You have to deal with increasing competition. Other tech savants in this industry provide optimum services at competitive rates.

There is a need to purchase and maintain tech equipment.

You may need a business license.

What does this term mean? Tech savants are tech-savvy. In other words, they love and spend most of their time on computers and other technological systems.

Types of Businesses

There are tech businesses you can start under $500. These services include managed IT service, on-demand IT, network setup, network security, cloud computing, database management, computer repair, VoIP service, data storage, and software support.

Managed IT Service

Regulated service providers are IT service personnel that work with small businesses. They provide services that target clients' company networks at a consistent rate. As time progresses, these companies spend less to maintain their networks, as there are fewer problems that will arise.

On-demand IT

Another tech business start-up worth commencing tech services on demand. There are several specific functions you can offer. Clients don't have to pay regular monthly fees. They can pay for individual services provided.

Network Setup

It also provides you with a basic setup service for businesses looking to upgrade their networks. It is possible to offer it as a discrete service, but it may be more valuable as part of the IT package it operates.

Network Security

Cybersecurity is a major concern for all businesses. So, assessing and responding to potential threats is a well-known service for most IT businesses. You can offer this as one of the limited IT offer services. But some businesses offer it as a separate service.

Cloud Computing

This category includes any type of IT service provided through the Internet or a dedicated cloud network. So, cloud platform or SASS submission falls into this category. So basically, you can create a kind of software that is distributed to users through the cloud and charge a membership fee to access it.

Database Management

Several businesses have databases that help owners and administrators manage business records. Some of these systems are small and simple, while others are large and intricate.

As a tech-driven entrepreneur, your role may include managing clients' sales, finances, and customer/employee information. This career path also includes overseeing compliance, security, and performance of data-based applications.

Software Support

Software support includes managing software products. These include spreadsheets, databases, or multimedia. A tech savant role in this field is to provide a service that supports customers who need technical solutions. You can focus on a list of specific types of software or programs or provide a more generalized service.

Computer Repair

Your discipline may not center on software engineering or networking. You may have a knack for hardware installation and maintenance, including devices like motherboards, computers, and graphics cards.

As such, there are business opportunities in this field. Individuals and entities alike need such services and are willing to pay significantly for them. Often, the tech savant has physical contact with the clients to identify and address their business needs.

In pursuing this path, it is essential to focus on the target market in one's local community.

VoIP Service

Voice over Internet Protocol (VoIP) is a platform that enables users to communicate with others using broadband internet connections rather than the traditional phone line.

Several on-demand voice-calling services provide a

sustainable source of income. Being an IT expert, this is an opportunity to launch a lucrative career with less capital.

Data Storage

Individuals and business entities deal with information daily. They need to store data. However, some of the data platforms available (especially the free versions) are not sufficient enough to handle a vast amount of data.

Besides, this discipline demands a sufficient level of knowledge and skill. Providing data storage services include creating a cloud platform or on-premises storage option for system backup or additional storage.

So, users do not need to store everything on their main devices. If you manage sensitive or proprietary data, you can combine this with a security offer.

How to Sell It

Is it possible to start a tech business with less than $500? The answer is yes, but conditional. You have to look in the right direction. To begin with, check out the average survival rate of a start-up. This figure is pegged at 10%.

That means that 90% of start-ups crash before they attain sustainability. Several factors account for this outcome. About 50% of these enterprises and businesses fail because the owners don't have relevant products to offer. For some, capital is the problem, while others don't have the right human resource.

With the knowledge of these stats, you can avoid major pitfalls. Your game plan should include creating, marketing, and selling a technological piece that is relevant to your target audience. By doing so, your new enterprise has a surviving chance.

What is the first step to launching a tech business?

Create the minimum viable product (MVP) needed by the market

Ensure that the product is verifiable by your initial clients

Make necessary modifications to make the product fit for the right market

Create a team of experts to oversee various aspect of the business

Get the funds required for business expansion

Develop and practice a dynamic approach towards business sustainability

Create a funding team

To be financially successful with a tech enterprise, an entrepreneur needs a ready market, one willing to purchase the tech products available. There is also the need to address customer grievances and understand the fair price for one's market. These are just a few of the things such an individual needs to know.

Start-ups based on user feedback from a constantly evolving app work best when repeatedly growing. If you intend to create a lean start-up, avoid the trap of registering an LLC. This prevents needless legal luggage.

You can go into business with a public partnership and co-founder. This will reduce your costs and protect you from problems such as organizational structure and taxes before selling the product. Technology occupies a top priority, even above the structures on which it stands.

Your product is what you are going to earn; above all, start with construction. Your fundamental skills are enough to set your home start-up off the ground.

You can lay the foundation for a new tech startup with an arbitrary foundation that allows you to pay bills for everyday work. As such, you have a sample that other co-founders can use.

If you are a non-tech entrepreneur building a tech business, you have to explain your vision in detail to the would-be CTO (Chief Technology Officer). This individual has in-depth knowledge on how to actualize your vision. In the same vein, you will be spending less.

How can you proceed with your tech start-up?

Analyze the main features of your product.

Most newbie entrepreneurs struggle to come up with ideal solutions to get their businesses sailing.

The key to creating an MVP is centering it around your own pain. What if other individuals share this pain and seek a solution? In this case, you can include the initial clients to revise the value proposition.

It is essential to explain the features, gather feedback and verify the business idea. As such, you can be sure that the final product heads in the right direction. Based on the report that 42% of failed start-ups stem from product/market incompatibility.

For this reason, information selection is essential for business survival. Have a simple framework that helps you to identify and analyze user goals. At the same time, find out how varying pain points align with the following:

The overall concept

The target audience

The end-users

Their needs

The aim behind the product (product goals)

Interestingly, building a minimum viable product comes with several choices. Your target should center on providing customers with the minimum features needed to achieve your value or goal.

Building a small start-up implies starting fast. A minimum viable product does not necessarily have to serve several audiences and use cases. You need a niche. Source for a small but high-target segment of your market to buy into the concept.

You also need to get the money to develop MVP and push it to the main market. One of the pitfalls to avoid is selecting the wrong market segment. Know the target audience to sell to create your minimum viable product that fits market demand.

In modifying your tech start-up, bring in your initial clients to build an engagement community. This group will provide feedback. Avoid following the wrong section as it prevents you from creating the time and insight to sustain the business. Business turnover cannot be realized if the MVP is not substantial.

Without verifying the MVP, a start-up tech savant only incorporates the shortcut to building a client-base, not the business model.

You could have a large audience and competitive business tools but still, flop in sustaining your business.

Your MVP is the pivot to business growth and sustainability.

Pre-sell your minimum viable product.

Many business owners with failing start-ups have one thing in common – lack of funds. They run out of money to sustain the product and, in turn, the business. One way to address this challenge is to bring paying customers on board quickly. These individuals become stakeholders who will benefit from the product's success.

In other words, they are co-developers. They provide financial support in exchange for the features requested. Most likely, these individuals will pay for the final product as well.

The sales of such tech products depict validation – your co-developers trust these products. What MVP strategies can you incorporate into your start-up?

Single-feature MVP, which focuses on nailing the client's goal to verify feature requirements and create initial adoption.

Piecemeal MVP reduces costs by compounding both existing products and services with a unique offer.

Concierge MVP automates the manual process that comes with operating specific software. Users can learn how best to work with such products.

Wizard of Oz MVP tends to look like a service. However, it contains a manual process that derives results. You can analyze the result generated by your software and validate its monetization (the users that pay to use it).

Crowdfunded MVP is another strategy that helps you create buzz and get feedback on a product before commencing production. This strategy reduces costs while generating finance to run the business and maintain sustainable earnings.

Smoke test MVP verifies the demand for tech-savvy ideas by transmitting paid traffic to a pre-release signup page, which, according to its number, will help you rate the level of interest in the product.

Identify and hire experienced professionals.

You may not have the technical skill and experience. But that is not a problem. You can partner with a co-founder who is well-versed in the business application of technology. All you need is an ideal start-up idea and equity.

But how can an entrepreneur with less than $500 achieve

that? Sourcing talent does not necessarily require breaking the bank or emptying one's life savings. Several platforms bridge this gap, including VentureStorm.

What amount of equity do co-founders get under start-ups? Generally, the value ranges from 10% to 35%. It is worth noting that future investment will influence such equity. As such, CEOs may be taking significant risks when on the lookout for such investments.

Secure Clients

Having approved the MVP and have iterated with client input, the following stage is to deliver the item into a more extensive section of your objective target audience. It becomes possible to meet all the ideal objectives requested by your clients, with quite a few highlights.

However, on the off chance that nobody realizes your item exists, you will miss out to other competitors. Tech start-ups without enormous paid promotions will find it difficult to have venture budgets and an all-around sales team.

The absence of finances can be inconvenient for a start-up tech savant, yet not a game-ender. The individual needs to be scrappy. In other words, hard manual promotion is key in this situation, especially one that doesn't scale. Find out where clients are dominant online and be involved in their discussions.

Engaging Online Communities

Here is one thing most start-up entrepreneurs can't forget in a hurry – their first product launch. Perhaps, they never saw the tons of responses coming, which, in turn, created several server problems and, as such, disabled their online activities.

A highly engaging tech product that finds its way to top tech sites like Techcrunch.com or Thenextweb.com can pull more than 10,000 visitors to your website. Most entrepreneurs incorporate this strategy into their main content promotion and product launch.

You can get information on how well your application functions when used by genuine clients by creating an inflow of new users into the product funnel. As such, it is easy to note the changes the app requires with respect to the needs of these individuals.

Signups are awesome. However, they are just a fragment of the entire activity. There must be product adoption, or the consistent generation of revenue overtime will be truncated. Most failed start-ups have this challenge. In the same vein, information exchanges don't reveal the entire story. Your clients have to receive the product and adapt it to maintain steady revenue for business growth and sustenance.

As a tech savant building a small-scale enterprise, you should look into the following: active users, net promoter score (NPS), and retention rate.

Dynamic clients routinely get back to utilize your item. They constantly sign in and don't leave forever - they get a genuine incentive from the tech app and are perhaps the most important resources for your business. With this, tech savants must know how to calculate active users on their platform. How can they achieve this?

Dynamic clients are normally monitored based on timeframe. Along these lines, your month-to-month dynamic clients (MAUs) are the individuals who have signed in inside the most recent 30 days. Each application advances distinctive use frequencies.

Twitter trusts you utilize the application consistently, on the grounds that there's continually something new to see, and it brings in cash from promotion impressions.

For example, Sumo is a tool most users may have to utilize less. This is based on the fact that as soon as you've incorporated a pop-up form, you don't have to make daily adjustments. Also, there is less needed to sign into the application.

Software like Google Analytics can come in handy in helping you figure out your active clients. It is a free service. However, there are other paid platforms, including Mixpanel and Amplitude, that are available for use.

Calculating your active users involves using their IDs and event tracking.

Another area worth looking into is the net promoter score (NPS). Are your clients happy with using your application? Does your product provide optimum customer satisfaction? Having a feedback mechanism will help you find the right answers to these questions.

Your initial clients involved in product reviews are assets to your start-up. They provide direction in which you can steer your application. But that's not all – they also play a role in product marketing, taking the bulk of the process off your shoulders.

As such, you can record high-converting referrals consistently, with ratings clocking between 9 and 10. Those app users, ranging from 1 to 6 on the scale, are often critics who have one or more problems using your app. And then, there are individuals within the scale of 7 and 8. These people can fall on either side.

What is the essence of the net promoter score? This evaluation metric system gives you a comprehensive idea of how satisfied your clients are in using your product. As the score increases, so does the overall well-being of your client base.

To calculate your customer satisfaction rate, you need to deploy a net promoter score survey, preferably through a section of the application, via email, or in the feedback section of the app store, like Google Play Store or Apple Store app.

You can use NPS survey tools, like Wootric, Promoter.io, and Delighted. Survey ratings are from 1 to 10.

So, here is the formula to calculate your NPS:

NPS = (% of user responses with ratings 9 to 10) − (% of user responses with ratings 1 to 6).

When it comes to retention rate, even the smallest tweaks make a significant difference. How do you intend to build a sustainable client base? What parameters should be considered?

Retention rate measures the percentage of clients who sign into the application after signing up. It is not uncommon to find tech savants with low retention rates. This implies that only a handful of those who signed up on the platform still use the product offered.

In such a situation, the individual should channel more resources into retaining more customers than generating leads to prevent leakage. Besides, retaining a user is six to seven times less in cost than getting a new one.

Why waste money getting a user if such an individual will only stay on the platform for a couple of weeks?

Calculating Success

How can a tech savant calculate the retention rate?

This is done by subtracting the number of users at the end of a specific timeframe from new clients created in that period. The result derived is divided by the number of users at the start of that period x 100.

What timeframe is ideal for this calculation? Most entrepreneurs use 30 days. In analyzing the result generated, it is easy to detect the relation between user-profiles and their behaviors toward promoting retention. A client that brings in more people has higher tendencies of being retained than one who only views the product.

With the above-discussed factors, retention rates, NPS, and the rest are ideal in monitoring app performance. However, you may likely be overwhelmed by tons of data that it becomes difficult to use the right information to improve your product.

With client input and reports on key measurements like activation and retention, it's an ideal opportunity to make applications, highlight, and advertising iterations that influence your bottom line. This implies settling on choices dependent on restricted data and voices of a couple of devoted clients - it can feel like an act of pure trust; however, the old Facebook mantra of Move Fast and Break Things is as yet an important message for new tech companies.

As your start-up gains a strong foothold, your partners and application will expand. However, this can't be achieved without the right support system and internal processes. As such, you have to do the following:

Work in sprints

Prioritize user feedback logging

Disable campaigns and features that don't matter to successful app engagement.

Funding and Scaling Your Start-Up

Most new business owners make the error of imagining that funding and scalability is the first step to take in starting a business. This process should come later in the start-up venture.

What is the first step to take? Create a product with the right target audience in mind. Get early adopters and quickly iterate before executing an enormous scope go-to advertisement strategy.

That does not mean that business scalability is bad. However, this move can hurt a start-up when introduced too soon. One factor that can hurt such a business is scaling up on products that are financially draining without delivering optimum and relatable solutions. You will end up wasting resources.

As soon as you have validated your minimum viable product, seek funding by generating an active list of active paying clients and capitalizing on that. This will set your start-up aside from other competitors in search of investor capital.

There are several ways to source funds when creating a tech start-up: angel investor, crowdfunding, and accelerators.

Angel Investor

These individuals are regularly ex-organizers that have a blend of startup experience and huge loads of money from their last enormous exit.

Generally, angel investors put resources into organizations that have valuations of around $3m. The average contribution is pegged at $150,000.

Crowdfunding

Crowdfunding is one of only a handful few alternatives accessible in the beginning phases before a product creates genuine income.

It is easy to source funds using this strategy through the following channels:

IndieGogo

Kickstarter

Fundable

Another option to this is pre-selling the minimum viable product. If that doesn't align with your plan, you can sell a specific percentage of the start-up stock to investors.

Accelerators

These individuals offer resources that are beyond finances. They include business opportunities, connections, and mentoring that would some way, or another be unattainable for most new businesses.

Once an accelerator accepts a business owner's application for this funding option, the latter provide within 7% to 10% of the business equity in return for $25,000 to $125,000.

However, there is one non-profit funding community that takes 0% of equity – MassChallenge. It comprises law offices, PR firms, corporate executives, venture capital firms, marketing agencies, and angel groups.

As such, new start-up owners have everything needed to get their businesses off the ground. There are also training opportunities geared toward marketing, strategizing, and raising funds for the business.

In summary, starting a home-based tech business has its challenges. However, with the right guidance, you can operate one successful even with a budget size of $500. You can create an app or render IT services to businesses that require such.

As a recap, here are some of the things worth noting when starting this venture:

Identify your MVP, including its features, with respect to meeting clients' needs.

Pre-sell it.

Provide equity in exchange to build a solid business team, which will include your CTO and CEO.

Source for your first set of clients and improve your services using a feedback mechanism.

Analyze your performance report and pivot using ideal analytical tools.

Incorporate the agile methodology.

Funding and scalability are essential – don't forget this aspect.

You don't need all the money in the world to create a tech start-up, especially one on a small-scale. Start small and expand wide – that's the rule of thumb to building a successful business in this category. Also, as you progress, note the pitfalls to avoid.

It is worth remembering that only 10% of start-ups succeed. Hence, come up with a plan that puts your business in this category.

Estimated Earnings

How much can you earn as a tech savant with a business? The real question is this: what counts as profit?

Often, profitability hinges on finance – how much money a business makes. In analyzing the estimated earnings of a tech start-up, one has to consider the following:

The start-up break-even point. At this point, your business revenue generated equals your expenses. Your business is done losing cash. You can utilize a strategy when making monetary projections to ascertain this point ahead of time.

Ramen Profitability. What does this mean? At this phase, the start-up pulls in more revenue to support the business owner, provided that there are minimal expenses. Unfortunately, most start-ups don't get to this business stage.

Corporate Profitability. This term is relative to the business owner. For some, it involves one being able to repay debts with ease, earn substantial paychecks, and have enough left for savings.

For tech savants, a new business can fetch in earnings $50,000 or less. However, as more investment funds come in, the paycheck increases. However, this is not as straightforward as it seems. It is essential to ask the following questions:

What is the revenue-generating size of your tech start-up? Depending on the funds that go into running the business, what will you have left?

How long will it take before recording a break-even point? If your projected paycheck is $100,000 per year for the next five years before there is business profitability in the sixth year, then you should know that it can get higher than that during that timeframe.

What do your investors want in return for their investments? Of course, with more investments comes more earnings.

Are you spending more than what is required to grow the business? Remember, your start-up also needs funds to grow as you do. Strike a balance between both sides.

As you generate more sales from your tech products, so does your business revenue, and your income increases.

Chapter Nine: Jobs for the Organizing Guru

Business Description

An expert coordinator transforms mess and confusion into a proficient space for families and organizations. The roles in this profession range from sorting out a pantry in a residential apartment to planning an extra room for an advertising firm.

Since tossing things out can be hard for customers,

organizing coordinators regularly need to likewise go about mentoring and assisting customers with analysis on their behaviors and responses around objects.

Further, coordinators need to find out about their clients to map out organizational systems they can implement successfully.

Coordinators might be associated with a portion of the craftsmanship, yet they regularly give enormous errands, for example, interior décor or construction projects, to subcontractors.

It is worth noting that such professionals are not mandated to obtain licenses to operate this task. However, there are organizations responsible for overseeing the affairs of organizing contractors. For example, the National Association for Professional Organizers provides interested individuals with courses in this area.

Homeowners tend to have several challenges in their homes. These may include:

Finding the ideal space for closets and other appliances.

Struggling with clutter around the apartment, including unused items.

Having too many clothes and shoes in one's closet.

Finding it difficult to keep belongings organized.

These factors are not limited to the home alone. Office spaces suffer cluttering as well. As such, there is a high demand for decluttering and organizing services.

Storage limitation is a problem as most average homes have less space to take more items. Apart from this problem, the concept of materialism is prevalent in many households. People buy what they don't need. For this reason, they have too much stuff.

As an organizing guru, you can help your clients screen their possessions and group each item batch in its respective category for proper storage. This includes:

Locating an ideal place in the apartment to keep items.

Finding individuals and entities that need such items, including charity organizations.

Disposing of such items (the last option)

You can help these individuals to reorganize their storage space. Such a service requires a practical and economical approach. Managing too many items is already a burden. Hence, there is a need to declutter the area of concern.

Proficient coordinators are typically individuals who are profoundly coordinated themselves. They have a skill for realizing where everything goes to appreciate adhering to the framework they have made.

On the off chance that you are one of these profoundly coordinated individuals, and you're additionally keen on helping other people arrive at a similar degree of professionalism, starting a private company as an expert coordinator might be an amazing business cut out for you.

Proficient coordinators can work with different individuals and organizations to help them wipe out their collected mess, get coordinated, and make a framework for overseeing records or assets going ahead.

Often, this is no walk in the park, particularly for the individuals who are not coordinated accordingly, making this a possibly rewarding business thought on the possibility that you have what it takes to dominate in this field.

You can work with homeowners, local entrepreneurs, and organizations. Here is the thing that you need to know before commencing your organizational and decluttering start-up.

Part of this service includes:

Consultation

Inventory

Arrangement and movement of items

Design layout

Implementation, and perhaps,

Moving services

Pros and Cons

Pros:

Your objective market can be broad.

You needn't bother with a particular license or training to be an expert coordinator.

You can acquire a feeling of achievement by helping other people get coordinated and showing them how to look after their items.

You can assist individuals with chronic disorganizations and other related problems.

You can provide services by sorting a section of a

business or home at a time.

There is a ton of data and tutorials on organizational systems and methodologies accessible on the web.

Cons:

The competition often tends to be generic. There may be little or nothing that makes your start-up stand out from the rest – technically speaking.

The organizing guru needs to get used to disorganized and cluttered spaces, including residential apartments and offices.

This profession requires a high level of empathy and patience. You have to be tolerant with your clients and avoid being disgusted at the slightest clutter you see.

It requires identifying your client's comfort level. This encapsulates both the individual's digital and physical organization.

To remain in the competition, you may have to get tons of certifications from reputable organizations.

Start-Up Costs

The start-up cost for this business depends on several factors. However, it is affordable. But here is a breakdown showing what to expect when setting sail with your decluttering and organizational start-up. You should consider:

Business registration

Domain name registration and website building

Legal documentation and fees

Logistics

By conducting a comprehensive search on these areas and many more, you can get the best deal.

How to Sell It

Professionalism is important.

You need a significant level of professionalism to stay relevant. Although this is not compulsory, it is recommended. Go through professional organizing books and websites. This shouldn't be limited to cluttering as you have to identify the needs that are out there.

Peruse blog entries from business owners, employers, homeowners, and other individuals and corporations to determine the difficulties faced in their work or residential environments.

Networking association is essential as well. Find an ideal organization to be a part of; for example, the Institute for Challenging Disorganization (ICD) or the National Association of Productivity and Organizing Professionals (NAPO). There might be a local chapter near you.

You don't have to spend a dime doing this. Conduct statistical surveying — attempt to pinpoint the kinds of customers you'd prefer to work with. Think about building up a specialty or specialized topic.

Create a Business Name

Your business name represents your start-up. In other words, it is the face of your company. As such, Create an extraordinary and unique name for your business and possibly a slogan, as well. Find out if the domain name is accessible.

There are helpful domain name search sites like WHOis.net, GoDaddy.com, NetworkSolutions.com, Namecheap, and many more. You can also register your start-up domain name here.

Check your Secretary of State site to check whether your business name is accessible and how to continue with respect to petitioning for a DBA (Doing Business As).

Consider Legalities, Finances, and Logistics

Legalities

In truth, you need a marketing strategy to promote business visibility. And even though this doesn't gravitate towards business legalities, you need to have your business framework in order before launching the business. You have 4 choices: C Corporation, S Corporation, organization, or sole ownership.

Most expert organizers are sole owners. In addressing legal problems, it is essential to register the business name at any designated office. This can be based on the city and province. You can obtain drafting grants or licenses from such firms. There are third-party full-service legal and business entities available as well, including BizFillings.

Identify the fee prerequisites for your state and apply for charge excluded status (if necessary) with your state's Department of Revenue. At the same time, purchase business protection (general obligation, home, and business hardware, mistakes, and exclusions).

Finances

When your enlisted organized start-up has been endorsed, complete the government SS-4 form and acquire a nine-digit EIN.

Ensure that you do this before setting up the business name. This is basic since it isolates business and individual accounting records. Get a business credit card or potentially Visa.

Make a financial plan and build up a daily practice for business responsibilities, including savings, recording costs, accommodating bank clarifications.

Select ideal accounting software and interface it with your financial balance. A perfect example is QuickBooks. So, what's next:

Map out a work area or office space for your professional organizer start-up.

Set up a mobile or telephone number and a suitable voice message.

You need a PC, supplies, and relevant business gear, including a printer and scanner.

Get a storage framework for your PC. This may include the likes of iCloud, Carbonite, Backblaze, and SugarSync.

Logistics

Make a rundown of services you'll offer and gauge your business costs. What will your rate be? Are you considering the hourly rate, project valuing, evaluation, retainer fee, and other estimations?

For business branding, you can create business materials utilizing Vistaprint or your nearby print shop. Branded items may include business cards, letterhead, and envelopes.

For more professionalism, and as highlighted before, you need a business website. You can build one yourself. There are several drag-and-drop web design sites, including Wix, WordPress, Joomla, and Weebly. If you can't build one, then hire a professional web developer who understands your business needs and can translate them into a captivating online business platform.

Your site pages should include Home Page, About Us, Contact, Testimonials, and many more. Make web-based media profiles on Instagram, Facebook, Twitter, Pinterest, or LinkedIn.

With these platforms, you can disseminate information about your service offer via social media posts. An invite letter and booking confirmation system will help create a seamless business process.

Estimated Earnings

The first question that comes to mind when starting a professional organizer business is this: how much should I set as my professional organizer fee? At what rate should my clients pay for my service?

Kindly note that that is no one-size-fits-all strategy in figuring out these rates? You have to consider your professional skills and experience to determine what you'll charge for your service. But that's not all there is to consider. Look into other aspects and calculate the price.

To begin with, the following questions come to mind.

What value are you providing?

We may need comprehension of the worth we give, and that will affect our capacity to set our costs. Arranging and organizing home and workspaces require creativity, which, when properly executed, is a win-win for both the entrepreneur and the client.

In the same vein, it creates a positive impact on the client's emotional, mental, and physical health. As such, you determine how much you intend to charge for your professional organizer services.

The work duration is a determinant in setting the rates. For example, for 40 hours a week, your fee may be $23 per hour. If you are working 30 hours a week, your fee may be $31 per hour.

You can set a rate of $47 per hour for 20 hours a week schedule. And if you are working 10 hours a week, you can peg your fee at $94 an hour.

Realizing these numbers additionally causes you to estimate the number of customers you need to select each month. This basic exercise causes you to gauge the amount you should charge, dependent on the amount you'd prefer to procure.

In any case, when your business begins moving, you'll have additional costs. This means that you should have a spreadsheet to include every single expense. As such, you have a vivid idea of the amount needed to sustain the business.

Before calculating your profits, look at the following expenses:

Business license

Taxes

Legal advice

Accounting

Property insurance (equipment) and business insurance

Financial expenses – bank charges and credit card processing fees

Professional associations – ICD, POC, NAPO, to mention a few

Conference

Coaching

Auto

Gas

Tolls

Car maintenance

Fines

Parking

Marketing (pictures, materials, social media platforms, graphic design, website development)

Stationery use in professional organizer projects.

Chapter Ten: Jobs for the Trendsetter

Business Description

As the world evolves, the way we transact business changes as well. New products and services flood the market daily. Successful entrepreneurs understand and anticipate current trends.

In the words of Napoleon Hill, "It is in the quiet that our best ideas occur to us. Don't make the mistake of believing that by a frantic kind of dashing around, you are being your most effective and efficient self. Don't assume that you are wasting time when you take time out for thought. Thought is the foundation upon which all else is built by man."

Creativity is what sets aside a start-up entrepreneur from the rest. Steve Jobs is a perfect example. To become a trendsetter, you should know your market niche.

Monitor the industry's best practices. In the same vein, identify your competitors' activities. This will help you plan and extemporize.

So, peruse magazines, newspapers, and blog entries. Watch online classes and attend conferences. Track patterns with Google Trends, Feedly, or Mashable.

Talk with your customers, companions, clients, contenders, and collaborators. Trendsetters know the trends. They can read market behavior and business lifespan.

By identifying these traits, you can project trend changes

to optimize your business profit. In truth, there will always be consumers in the market. However, to attract these individuals is to think like one.

So, what product and service would you love to enjoy? How would you want it? These are questions worth asking. Don't overlook the place of building a customer-centric culture in creating a business opportunity. You should make your clients fall in love with your product and service.

Top trendy business ideas and innovations stem from reacting proactively to clients' necessities. Keep in mind the relationship you share with your devoted client-base.

They provide reliable feedback and rating that will help you as a start-up entrepreneur improve your product and service.

According to Walt Disney, "Do what you do so well that they will want to see it again and bring their friends."

Launching a new product or service can either make or break a start-up. For this reason, you must be creative.

Channel your resources and time to align your business with defined trends. Bring in a fresh perspective on what your business has to offer.

Pros and Cons

Pros:

You can make an accurate forecast of the business market using trends. Trendsetters can predict the future of their start-ups using specific parameters.

Trend-setting places you on the pedestal of leadership. Your thoughts and actions become critical to business growth, team coordination, and customer satisfaction. In other words, you can set the pace.

It helps you generate profitable business ideas.

You can spot warning signs or red flags earlier than others.

Cons:

> With trend-setting, indicators used cannot detect if the market profitability is short-term or long-term, which may affect decision making.

> Following business trends rashly can lead to losses, which can destroy a start-up's existence.

> Skipping some trends to avoid unforeseen circumstances may lead to a start-up entrepreneur missing out on big business opportunities.

How to Sell It

Before discussing how to launch a start-up as a trendsetter, understand that channeling all resources on trends can hamper business growth and sustainability. This can be compared to monitoring the FX market.

To optimize business profitability, you have to catch the wave from the onset, not half-way or at high points when the momentum is almost exhausted.

The last thing you need is to purchase several trendy products at high price points only to sell them for less the purchasing cost or at a discount. This is one way for your business to fizzle out. You should not purchase high and sell low.

A profitability trend showcases the direction of profit in a business. An upward trend implies that profit has commonly expanded after some time in the short or since quite a while ago run.

A descending profitability trend implies profits are declining. Perceiving issues from the get-go in profitability trends gives you a superior opportunity to address income and cost issues in play.

Catching trends at the right time can be financially rewarding. For example, some years back, fidget spinners were in high demand, creating a lot of buzz on several online platforms. People who sold this product made significant profits. Fast forward to today, anyone with a large stock of this item may have a tough time sustaining the business as it is no longer in vogue.

Trends are profitable based on the market niche. If you are into entertainment, fashion, food, tourism, and the likes, you can build a trendy business. How are demand cycles developed?

You need to evaluate the steps taken by large entities in repurposing and repositioning "out-of-fashion or old products" and make them the "in-thing." Finding the right spot to ride the wave of a fad is key to building a trend-setting business. Here are guides to effectively exploiting trends to become a successful start-up trendsetter:

Find a trend that aligns with your start-up. As brazen as it may seem, several small and large-scale entities root for diversification in pursuit of profit generation that never existed. This is more like chasing a bag of gold at the end of a rainbow. Remember, all that glitters is not gold. You should know what your clients want before creating a synergy between your start-up and the respective trend.

Ensure that your product costs are low and margins are high. This is better than riding the wave of a trend midway. You can't buy high and sell low with the expectation of growing your business successfully. This works best in an environment that supports significant product demand and exclusivity.

One secret to creating a successful trend-setting business is to procure products and services at a low-cost point. As such, you can easily generate significant profits, which can be reinvested.

Even when the price momentum ends, you can still retain substantial revenue. One thing you should bear in mind when riding trends is that they don't last forever.

Every trend has its start point and endpoint. As such, you should have more to offer your clients. This could be in the form of opportunities or promotions. Also, learn to move in and out of a trend. Don't overstay your business presence in a particular trend.

Not all trends are worth taking. Some are dead ends that will only stall business growth. Understand your market niche and restructure your start-up to take advantage of the next wave.

Despite what might be expected, a setup business may

have produced a profit in a new period, while its new profitability trends raise doubt about its future practicality. High-demand products and management help trendsetters drive income, which, joined with successful monitoring of expenditure, create profitability.

There are three types of profitability levels. They include working, gross, and net. Operating profit is gross profit subtracted from overhead. Net profit is the amount earned after removing expenses from the gross profit.

Net profitability is essential to accomplishing revenue-driven business goals. In any case, net profit trends are regularly a solid sign as to bigger business profitability. In the event that you have high gross profit edges, you have a superior opportunity to cover overhead and bring in cash.

Inner Trends

Inner trends involve the adjustment of profitability within a time frame. In some cases, a trendsetter's start-up gross profit may experience a decline consistently. This may stem from increased expenditures and a short inflow of revenue.

On the other hand, an upward gross profit trend shows a steady increase in income and start-up financial status. If operating and net profit trends decrease, the trendsetter may likewise need to survey fixed and irregular expenses.

Industry Trends

It is worth noting that profitability trends are prevalent in start-ups as well. A declining trend that is a contrast to industry standards may pose a serious business challenge.

Perhaps, the start-up has demonstrated a 4% increment in gross profit for over two years, but the gross profit is on a sharp decline, then you have to examine the trend. Chances are that there is a conflict between the business and the trend.

On the off chance that the entire business experience a monetary slump, a more unassuming decrease in profitability for your business is sensible.

Types of Trendsetter Businesses

Trend-setting start-ups are gaining more popularity based on several factors, including technology. People are becoming more aware of the seamless effort it takes to create such businesses with less or no money.

Additionally, several businesses in varying industries have undergone downsizing as most operations are outsourced. As a result, the market is flooded with tons of contracting opportunities for experienced and skillful persons.

For example, freelance individuals have generated additional sources of sustainable income via creating and maintaining a home-based market. Unlike before, several start-ups can run smoothly in the present economy

You don't need to empty your purse to start a small business, especially one that gravitates towards trends. However, some factors may come into play when expanding the start-up, including payrolls, rent, and consulting fees. These elements may also determine one's revenue.

However, thanks to the ubiquity of some technology and its gadgets, many trending businesses have experienced less overhead costs — low start-up costs with high-profit margins.

Here are some trend-setting businesses you can start and their related expected earnings.:

Online influencer marketing. Many factors influence the earnings of an online influencer, including the amount of followership, engagement rate, niche, platform, and the influencer's expertise on selling trending ideas, products, and services to the market. Some influencers make anywhere between thousands of dollars to millions of dollars yearly. For example, in 2017, PewDiePie, the notable YouTube influencer, made a whopping $12 million.

Social media marketing. On average, social media marketers who are trendsetters make $50,000 yearly, without spending up to $500 for their campaign setup.

Recruiting. The average earning of a professional in this field is $49,315 per year.

Tutoring. As a trend-setting tutor, your average earning sits between $25 to $60 per hour. Some tutors charge more.

Business consulting. These individuals are aware of business trends and understand how to stay ahead of the game, providing a trail-blazing path for other business owners. Yearly earnings of business owners range from $60,839 to $90,386.

Digital marketing. This is another field that often centers on business trends. What's new? Digital marketers earn between $40,000 and $97,000 per year.

Blogging – the king of trends. To be a blogger, you must understand the trends. In other words, you have to keep abreast of the latest to provide your target audience with evergreen content. Interestingly, individuals in this field can make anywhere between $100 and $25,000 per sponsored post.

It is worth noting that the cost of start-up for these professions is relatively low. However, they provide end-users with a value proposition. In other words, such a target audience can enjoy convenience and speed. Some of these businesses are mainly remote-based.

Other businesses not listed above, including dog training, may require the trendsetter to commute to different destinations via a personal transport system. Most of these professionals offer home-based services, creating an amazing customer experience.

For some professions, these trendsetters may have to obtain specific licenses and permits to operate.

Freelancers providing business-to-business services can target small and mid-scale enterprises in need of third-party professionals but have less budget size to keep them on the payroll full-time.

Being a trend-setting freelancer, you have the platform to handle a reasonable amount of clients to work with. In most cases, such jobs are done remotely. As such, this field extends beyond an individual's geography. Some trend-setting freelancers include:

Copywriters

Blockchain technology experts

Data scientists

Social media managers

Graphic designers

Online educators

Speaking of the last profession (online educators), there is a surge in the number of professionals providing end-users with skill learning services. In fact, this is a top-profitable online business anyone with knowledge in specific areas can venture into and earn a significant income.

You can provide virtual instructions, create online courses, and manage training schedules via online companies like Udemy. One strong point that comes with this profession is the ability to telecommute. You can work from home with less start-up cost.

Drop-shipping and affiliate marketing have been on the rise. Best still, they come with almost zero-cost for setup. To make a difference in these areas, a trendsetter must understand market trends. What do people want per time? And how can we make such products and services available on time?

Surprisingly, most small start-ups are online-based because it takes fewer resources to run while promising significant returns. Often, all you need is a PC or a smartphone, an internet connection, and other peripheral devices.

You don't have to bother about renting an office space or coping with outrageous utility bills in your corporate environment.

It is no news that trendsetters have been able to create six-figure businesses out of thin air. They know where to look into and what to look out for.

Most high-profitable start-ups are those with potential high margins. Unlike the traditional corporate world that expands on the element of scalability, trendsetting businesses focus on maintaining a significant percentage share of the profit made on each transaction, with some being above 15%.

As such, trendsetters are self-supportive. Creating a start-up in this field does not necessarily involve you taking an all-or-nothing approach. You can start a part-time trendsetting business while overseeing your nine-to-five job. You only need to understand and optimize your business market niche and take action at the right time.

Chapter Eleven: Jobs for the Outdoorsy

Business Description

A recreational vehicle (RV) rental business gives reasonable choices to individuals hoping to lease different types of RVs, ranging from Type A motorhomes to pop-up trailers.

Rentals are an engaging choice for those clients who appreciate tourism, exploration, and unique transportation within a location, in an RV but don't prefer the responsibility of commuting in a personal or public vehicle.

What are the benefits of RV rentals for these individuals?

In the time past, leasing an RV came with an incredible challenge for holidaymakers and travelers. Customers' requests were limited within their zones, and they needed to contact RV agencies to get RVs for their necessities.

One needed to manage high rental charges and oppressive salesmen who often thought less about clients' RV needs.

Because of online evolution and business development, it is currently simple for travelers to scout for boundless RV alternatives and schedule their RV trips, all from the solace of their homes. For this reason, large numbers of these rental organizations offer shared rental platforms; this implies that RV proprietors can lease their vehicles to others.

Holidaymakers and travelers who intend to enjoy amazing camping trips in their RVs can rent one, especially if such events occur fewer times. Opting for this option provides them with the platform to drive such vehicles without bearing the burden of ownership, which includes maintenance.

If you own an RV, this is an opportunity to create a start-up and earn additional income. There is a high demand for such services, and the market is becoming more competitive by the day.

Pros and Cons

Pros:

> You are in control of your business and resources, including time, money, effort, and will.

> RV rental businesses can fetch a significant amount of money. It is no news that most RV owners make tens of thousands of dollars yearly; some make way more.

> You have a sense of business security.

RV businesses give you the platform to work from anywhere in the world.

It provides a change of scenery as you are not transfixed on one spot, unlike the brick-and-mortar business.

It requires low-cost to start up.

You can advertise your business without spending much money.

Cons:

Sometimes, the costs that come with the business can be overwhelming. These include insurance, maintenance, storage, and many more.

Unexpected repairs can take a toll on your RV business.

Regardless of the expenses that come with running an RV business, you can cater to them from the profits made via rentals if you position your start-up correctly.

Start-Up Costs

Creating an RV business comes easy when you already have an RV for rent; otherwise, you may need to purchase one. Here are some of the prices attached to different RV types:

Class A Motorhome (Diesel) - $230,000 to $1,000,000+ (New)/$35,000 to $500,000+ (Used)

Class A Motorhome (Gas) - $105,000 to $200,000 (New)/$20,000 to $150,000 (Used)

Class C Motorhome - $45,000 to $95,000 (New)/$12,000 to $80,000 (Used)

Fifth Wheel Trailer - $40,000 to $160,000 (New)/$15,000 to $115,000 (Used)

Travel Trailer - $15,000 to $80,000 (New)/$8,000 to

$60,000 (Used)

Interestingly, some RVs cost way less than the figures specified above. However, you have to examine them thoroughly before committing to your finances. The next area to look into is the cost of maintenance.

On average, expect to pay an average amount of $117.52 per month on keeping the RV in good condition. The average yearly cost may be pegged at $1,410.20.

How to Sell It

You have discovered the ideal start-up idea. Now you are prepared to make the following stride. The first step to take is to enlist the RV rental business with the state. In this section, there is a step-by-step guide to help you actualize your start-up goals.

By following them, you can plan and register your RV start-up and prepare for unforeseen circumstances. In achieving this, consider the following:

Business name and registration

The start-up and operational cost

Your target audience

Rental rates

The previous section covers some part of the start-up costs for an RV business. It is worth noting that for this profession, the costs are typically higher.

However, if you are taking over an already established rental business, you may spend fewer resources. You can start your business with one RV and then acquire more as it grows. In the same vein, it is essential to have a business and personal liability insurance policies in place.

Other factors to consider are business marketing and online presence. The latter entails building a website for your rental business. Online visitors in need of a recreational vehicle for tourism or camping can book one on your site with ease.

But this doesn't come on a platter of gold. You need to invest in advertising the RV business to create visibility.

Source for financing and investment avenues. This can be done personally or with the help of a professional like a certified accountant or lawyer.

If you have an RV, then good for you. Your start-up costs will be greatly reduced. All you have left is to advertise your business to attract clients.

Apart from the cost of maintenance and upkeep, there are other expenditures you may undertake. For example, your RV will need new tires. There will be wheel balancing and alignment from time to time. How about regular tune-ups, part replacement, and oil changes.

The next area to consider is your target audience. Who are they? Are you considering individuals, couples, or families?

Your target niche should comprise people who spend more time enjoying outdoor activities but also need a home-away-from-home experience. A recreational vehicle provides them with this luxury and comfort.

Determine your rates. How much do you want to charge by night? It is worth noting that prices are dependent on the RV class – Class A, B, C, and others. Also, additional amenities can influence this element. Used RVs can cost $100 to $200 per night. On the other hand, a new one may take an additional $100 or $200, depending on the features it possesses.

To fix your price, you have to research the market. Know what other RV owners are charging within your location.

Creating a Business Name

Picking the correct business name is essential but at the same time tasking. In the event that you don't, as of now, have a name, you can use an RV Rental Business Name Generator.

If you control a sole proprietorship, then consider creating a business name that differs from yours. Here is a guide on searching for the ideal name for your start-up. Go through the following:

Federal and state trademark records

State's business records

Web domain availability

Social media platforms

Several domain sites help you will available business names, including GoDaddy.com. In the same vein, create a professional email account (@yourcompany.com).

What legal approach do you want to take in setting up your business? Here some business structure types:

Partnership

Sole proprietorship

Corporation

Limited liability company (LLC)

The last two options are ideal and can keep you protected from legal issues in your RV rental business. Creating an LLC comes with low state costs. Another option is to hire a formative business service.

Get a registered agent for your LLC. Some of its packages include the implementation of registered agent services of up to a year.

You can get a registered agent or become one.

Kindly remember that taxes are unavoidable, including those on a state or federal level. It is important to undertake this task before launching your start-up. But first, apply for an employer identification number (EIN). Getting one is straightforward.

The IRS online platform is one of the means through which you can obtain your EIN; options include fax or email.

Get a Bank Account

To protect your personal assets and separate them from your business assets, have a dedicated banking account that handles all business transactions.

If there is a legal issue, you won't risk losing your home, cars, or other valuables.

This option also provides you with an avenue to build an ideal business credit, which opens your start-up to more funds in its name, not yours. Furthermore, you get high lines of credit, significant interest rates, just to mention a few.

Having a business account helps you to conduct auditing and tax filing with ease. You can record your expenditures and revenues easily. With this, it is easy to monitor your start-up financial performance. Your accounting record remains accurate, simplifying your annual tax filing.

Licensing and Insurance

Your business may be slammed with hefty fines if you skip this option, causing it to fizzle out. What are your local and state requirements in getting these legal documents?

Kindly note that operating an RV rental business comes with legalities. If you are operating your physical location, it is essential to obtain a Certificate of Occupancy (CO). This establishes the fact that your business has met the following.

Zoning laws

Building codes

Government regulations.

When leasing a location, ensure that the landlord can obtain a valid CO for the RV rental business. Besides, the individual is responsible for getting one.

It is worth noting that a new CO is also required after a major renovation. If the location used is undergoing renovation, you should specify that lease payments will be halted until you get a valid CO.

What if you want to build or buy a business site for operation? In that case, you are to personally get a valid CO from the designated local office. But that's not all. Go through the requirements for building codes and zoning with respect to the business site.

Is your start-up well protected? What happens when legal issues or disasters arise? You have to factor in these elements to have a smooth-running business.

Why is business insurance important? For one, it protects your start-up finances should there be an unfortunate financial event. Operating an RV business comes with several risks. As such, you need the right insurance policy to keep it safe.

Some of these risks are unanticipated – we don't see them coming. So, what do you do in such situations? You can get General Liability Insurance. Most business owners opt for this policy for a start.

Over time, you may need more hands on deck. Having Workers' Compensation Insurance will help you cater to your employees.

Creating a Unique RV Rental Brand

How can you stand out from other RV business owners? Brand statement. Your brand is the face of your start-up. This determines the way the public views your business.

To have a strong business presence, your branding must be top-notch. In creating a good brand, the following comes into play:

First, your business logo must be on point. If you are a graphic designer, then this is an opportunity to channel your skills and experience into creating the perfect logo, contact card, brochure, flyers, and other materials for your RV rental business. Otherwise, you may have to hire a professional.

The next step is to promote and market the start-up. Networking comes into play as it gives you a platform to reach out to a wider audience through RV booking platforms – an example being Outdoorsy. Of course, this option comes with applicable fees. Nevertheless, it is an ideal way to get more attention and engagement.

Such platforms also increase business visibility. Have your social business accounts ready. These include Instagram, Twitter, and Facebook accounts. But remember, the place of a business website cant be compromised as it showcases professionalism and builds trust in the hearts of online visitors.

Having an online presence gives customers the opportunity to know more about your services.

Your designed flyers should not be nestling on your desk. Get them busy. Distribute them at several RV campgrounds and parks within and outside your vicinity. These materials contain your business services, location, and other offerings.

Don't hesitate to get the word out.

Retaining Your Clients

Understand that your business reputation is always on the line. So, you should ensure that you make the right call at all times. Your RV services should be transparent and straightforward to your clients. Ensure the RV is clean and well-maintained to serve the next renter conveniently.

You can also provide these individuals with park guides and travel packages that will make their stay a memorable one. Incentives are great as well. They may include reduced pricing for loyal customers.

You may offer discounts for reviews or testimonials. By doing so, you build retention.

If you are using the RV personally for a particular business, then you can consider the following products and services.

Advertising sales

Accounting and tax preparation

Business or life coach

Antique dealership

Computer training and technical support

Computer programming

Auto detailing and RV cleaning

Jewelry designing

On-site massage therapy

Mobile auto/RV repair

Catering services

Is RV rental services a call in the right direction? This question has several depending factors. You should have good communication skills. Be willing to talk to people, letting them in on your business offering. Additionally, know the state and national park rules and regulations for RV camping.

Estimated Earnings

How much can you make from an RV rental start-up? The profit generated depends on the number of RVs in operation and the expenses incurred. Generally, you could have an annual earning ranging from $5,000 to $30,000.

You can improve your business profitability by renting out RVs during special events, including festivals, concerts, and sporting events.

In truth, not everyone fancy hotel reservations or Airbnb bookings. Some want to enjoy the thrill of enjoying their camping trips from a vehicle. They wish to enjoy the luxury of their homes while mobile. Short-distance booking can cut down on your RV's mileage.

Chapter Twelve: Jobs for Mr. and Mrs. Fix It

Business Description

Are you good are providing cleaning and maintenance services? Is there anything you can organize or repair, whether it is in an office or residential environment? Then you can start a "Fix It" business. Business owners and homeowners have items that need repairing, replacement, or servicing.

You can set aside a work schedule to attend to these cleaning and maintenance needs. This could be daily, weekly, or monthly.

Why physical presence and engagement is unavoidable, you can create an online to handle requests and other necessities, saving you money, time, effort, and other resources.

Perhaps, a business owner's office space encountered a disaster, like flooding, and such an individual is in need of a professional cleaning service. You can render your skill and experience in resolving such needs.

What services can you provide?

Hard floor maintenance

Door repair

Floor and window care

Ceiling fan repair

Restroom cleaning and repair

Furniture cleaning or repair

Deck and patio repair

Faucet repair

Electrical repair

Kitchen repair

Lighting fix

Plumbing maintenance

These are a few of the many services you can offer as a "fix-it" business owner. Your repair and maintenance service may center around office suites, multi-tenant buildings, corporate environments, retail spaces, educational environments (high schools and colleges), concert halls, construction sites, sports arenas, and architectural studios.

Pros and Cons

Pros:

Your overhead costs are, for the most part, low.

Your startup costs are low, provided that you have the apparatuses and gear required.

It's a great business with low maintenance costs.

You have the potential to make high-margin profits.

The business is scalable.

You can specialize. For example, you can decide to partner with realtors or work on commercial buildings alone.

Get more referrals via referrals and word of mouth.

You have tons of franchise opportunities at your

fingertips.

Cons:

You may have to obtain a contractors' license

Procuring business licenses in some locations can be difficult due to the stringent requirements that come with them

Some handyman projects are seasonal

You have to physically and mentally fit

Building the business to a break-even point can be a bit time-consuming

You should be knowledgeable and experienced in remodeling, home construction, maintenance, and repair.

You have to take your time to build a significant client base

You need liability insurance

You should have a complete set of work tools to undertake each project.

Start-Up Cost

It is worth noting that creating a handyman start-up is cost-effective compared to other start-ups. You don't have to break the bank or empty your life savings. It gets better if you have the skills and tools required to get started.

But here is the thing you may not know. This profession comes with several hidden costs. So, what should be expected before launching a Mr. and Mrs. Fix It business?

The good news is that you don't need to spend much if you have the tools, transport system and intend to market your business personally. In fact, with as little as $500, you can get your business up and running almost immediately.

Even though it is affordable, you shouldn't be frugal about getting your business in shape. This can slow down your business progress and cost you more over time.

Here is a breakdown of the costs you should expect and how to sell your business:

To get a business license, you may spend anywhere between $100 and $1,000, depending on your city and state of residence. You have to consider the plan and structure on which your business will run.

Are you considering sole proprietorship, S Corp, or LLC? How do you go about procuring and submitting the forms?

LLC filing may cost you $400 to $500. Even when filing with your state, you will pay a similar amount. However, it doesn't end at LLC. You may have to procure other business licenses.

You can get a city business license for your handyman start-up. The cost of this license is anywhere between $100 and $200.

Then there come your business cards. Designing and printing these cards can set you back $20 to $80. Note that the quality of your business card reflects your business standards. It speaks volumes about your professionalism. Hence, ensure that they look premium.

You have to rent a mailbox. Rentals can range from $125 to $250 for six months. This is an ideal option compared to using your home address. Anticipate this factor when creating your handyman start-up.

Create a business bank account. It will cost you $40. Setting up a bank account is a walk in the park. Your minimum balance of $25. The first 100 checks may need an additional $15 as the minimum.

Setting up accounting software is essential as well. Some systems are free, while others may be as high as $250. You need an accountant or a bookkeeper. Such services can be anywhere between $50 and $1,000. Expect an initial setup fee for bookkeeping services.

You have to plan out the cost of designing your handyman start-up website. The cost varies - $150 to $8,000. You can design your website with several drag-and-drop website builders, including Wix. If you are hiring a web designer to undertake the project, set aside about $2,000. This cost can increase depending on the individual or entity designing the site.

It is not mandatory to get a uniform. However, you have to be professional about your services, including appearance. This factor will influence how you charge your clients. Cost may range from $100 to $350. Other factors include:

Some logo designing applications are free. Others might set you back hundreds of dollars. You can choose between designing your logo personally or hiring a professional.

Opting for the latter will be an ideal option, except your skills in this field are top-notch. Logo design costs can be as high as $2,000, depending on your requirement and the professional.

Advertising Costs can also range from $0 to $2,000. Craigslist is an ideal place to market your handyman services. You don't have to pay to showcase what you do.

Not all advertising strategies work. Find the one that suits your business. But bear in mind that this involves testing several methods.

If you already have your tools, then you don't have to spend a dime. You can use them to carry out various projects. However, ensure that they are in good condition. If you don't have a set of tools, then you have to get one.

The price of purchasing these work items may be as high as $500, depending on what you are looking for.

Procuring a contractor's license. Such licenses vary depending on your business location and other factors – $0 to $4,000. In some states, you need this license to undertake handyman projects in any home. You have to find out if your state supports this before moving on with your business preparation.

As a handyman, you need insurance, but it may not be immediately. For this coverage, expect to pay $1,000 per year.

Of course, you want everything to reflect your handyman

business, including your van. You can brand it to showcase your business logo, services, and contact details. You may pay anywhere between $150 and $2,000.

What if you don't have the right knowledge to get started? In that case, you need training in this field. Some services range from $1,000 to $8,000. You can access courses, books, and other materials online. There are even online consultancy services available at affordable rates.

Kindly note that the knowledge acquired will generate you more profits over time.

Estimated Earnings

As a handyman living and working in the U.S., expect average annual earnings of $37,067. In that case, your average working hourly rate may be pegged at $17.82.

Some years back, the housing industry nose-dived due to the global recession. Homeowners and business owners cut down their expenses on specific services. Some paid less for household tasks, which were not mandatory.

However, in recent times, there has been a significant increase in the demand for handyman services. Global consumer confidence has bounced back. With the right business approach, you can make up to $3,000 per week.

Chapter Thirteen: Jobs for the Adviser

Business Description

A financial adviser business is a private start-up that you can launch from your home office or lease a sizeable business office.

Particularly with a maturing gen X-er populace, the demand for financial advisers is expanding – with more people interested in insurance, investments, and real estate.

With a background in finance and customer service, you can start a financial adviser business without spending a fortune.

The consensus is that the next decade to come or more will be more time-consuming for financial advisers as recent pension freedoms and other legislative changes create more complexity in pensions, taxes, and public finance planning.

Factoring in this and the allure of owning a financial planning start-up means that whether you are an experienced consultant or a newbie in this industry, the chances of starting your own financial consulting company look attractive. One thing is for sure, there is always room for quality business in the market.

But note that creating a financial planning business from scratch is no walk in the park. There are several costs to consider. But that is not the elephant in the room. You may have to deal with the ever-changing business regulations.

Most sole financial advisors struggle in that aspect. But with the right approach, you can build a sustainable business in this field. All you need is constructive planning and research. Also, be patient about the process. It won't happen overnight.

In setting your business right, you have to take into consideration your market niche and the cost. Identify that which you want to achieve in your business.

Pros and Cons

Pros:

Enhance customer experience by providing deeper engagement

Create an improved long-term client viability

Increase client-base

Implement work schedule flexibility

Enjoy unlimited creativity in providing financial services

Cons:

Gaining new prospects is challenging

You have to deal with diverse regulatory and compliance requirements

It is a stressful industry

Start-Up Costs

How much money is required to create a financial planning start-up? It is worth noting that the cost of this business can range from $10,000 to $20,000. Additionally, you should be a registered investment advisor. This is done at the state level. Starting a business is more than just registering in the state.

Some of the capital will go into renting an office space, processing legal documentation (fee disclosure and form

ADV client brochure), and paying vendor fees.

You should secure a suitable contract with a custodian. Here are some steps to ensure that your business is properly registered and set to commence.

Map out a plan for your business. Success as an entrepreneur requires a clear plan. It helps you to map out the features of your business and discover unforeseen circumstances.

What business name do you have in mind?

What is your target niche?

How much do you have for the start-up?

What is your rate?

Before starting a financial planning firm, you have to consider office maintenance. Other factors include:

Rent

Liability insurance

Account maintenance fees

Labor cost

Omissions insurance

What is your market niche? In other words, who makes up your target audience? Are you considering middle-income earners or upper-class individuals? Your target audience should be able to afford your services or invest in them.

Come up with an ideal name for your start-up. This can be challenging for a newbie. However, there are online name generators that can generate business names in a matter of seconds. This saves you time. To check name availability, you can go through the business records on the state's website or check federal and state trademark records.

Before proceeding with other activities, ensure that you secure your business domain name before anyone else.

There are domain registration online sites that help you generate business names, including:

Domain.com

HostGator

Namecheap

Buydomains

DreamHost

Take advantage of business email services, like Google's G Suite. Such platforms come with several applications, including spreadsheets and word processing.

Once done, create a legal entity. This could be any of the following – partnership, sole proprietorship, corporation, and LLC. As discussed before, creating an LLC protects personal assets in the event that the financial advisory faces a legal battle, the individual's properties remain intact.

Create your own LLC and pay only low state LLC costs or get a business formation service for a small additional fee. You should select a registered agent for your LLC.

Factor in the element of taxes. These include state and federal taxes. While at it, forward your application to get an EIN. This number is one of the requirements of tax registration. You don't have to pay a dime to undergo this process.

EIN application is available on the IRS website. You can also obtain it via mail or fax. Having this number comes with several merits, especially when creating an LLC.

Your business type determines the type of tax you'll pay. In the case of an LLC, it falls under the S Corp tax category. You may also have to pay state taxes, depending on your business location.

The financial services business usually consists of one or more financial advisors who help financial planners and individuals manage their money. Some financial services businesses specialize in certain areas, such as retirement planning, while others include public finance consultants who help manage assets, liabilities, and insurance in addition to setting and achieving financial goals.

Investigate other financial services businesses in your area. Find out what other financial services businesses do in one place. Take a look at the types of services these companies offer.

Review the company's website, print ads, brochures, and more to see how these companies reach potential clients. Investigate your state laws for financial services businesses. Most states require businesses engaged in financial services to obtain a business license.

Contact your State Finance Office or visit Business.gov to determine the state-specific information applicable to your business. For example, any business engaged in the money service business in Houston must submit a full licensing application.

Invest or get a legal license. If you want to sell stocks, bonds, mutual funds, and other investments to your clients, you need to get an investment license (Series 7) or an Insurance License (Series 65).

For financial services businesses that offer legal advice, you must also obtain a license to practice law. Write a business plan.

A business plan for a financial services business is a guide that determines the goals of the business, how the business works, and what kind of clients you have in your services.

A business plan also addresses the starting costs of your business, the business location of your financial services, and how you reach clients.

Set up your fees and services. Create a list of services you offer. Next to each service, list how you charge for the services. Financial services companies may charge a service-based fee, one percent of the business conducted for the client, or withholding or flat rate fee.

The financial planner is usually the owner of the financial advisory firm. As a CEO, you need to be comfortable working long hours, have a financial interest in everything, and a special interest in the human psyche.

Most financial decisions are not just about numbers. They are about the client's behavior and how he or she sees the world. For example, some investors are concerned about the environment and may refrain from investing in fossil fuels regardless of the long-term returns of mutual funds or stock investors.

Other investors may be more careful about protecting their principal and earning conservative returns. These investors are willing to invest only in bonds, bond funds, annuities, fixed life insurance, and conservative bank products.

Some clients may not be comfortable investing their money. Others may need help in spending, or they may focus on saving money, living a happier life, and they will come to you for advice on what to do.

Understanding the psychophysiology of different types of people and understanding how each of your clients relates to money can help them gain their trust and provide better services for their long-term financial gain.

Estimated Earnings

As a financial planner, you can generate revenue by charging clients for financial advice, modular plans, comprehensive plans, and even investment management. Generally, financial advisors take a percentage of the managed assets as their fees. This is typically between 1% and 2%.

Creating a comprehensive financial plan may set a client back $1,800 to $10,000, depending on the requirements. What makes financial advisory businesses lucrative is the high-profit margin. This can range from 10% to 20%.

Chapter Fourteen: Jobs for Creators and Creative People

Business Description

According to Jonathan Schattke, a notable scientist, "Necessity is the mother of invention, it is true, but its father is creativity, and knowledge is the midwife."

Ideas rule the world. However, for them to be effective, they are interlaced in creativity. Whatever exists around us stems from this element. Moving on to business, creating a start-up from home can be daunting, but will creativity, anyone can make it work.

Do you have a creative skillset that is in high demand (graphic design, content creation, mobile development, web design, and many more)? You can create a start-up based on such skills and market them to clients.

Other elements embedded in running a creative business include persistence, planning, skillset, and time investment. Of course, you have a passion, which you intend to monetize. You can turn it into a creative business.

With the internet evolution, you can run a full-time business remotely with less capital, few resources, and no inventory. You don't have to leave your couch to provide customers with the right service.

Pros and Cons

Pros:

Provide creative business solutions that address the needs of a wide target audience

It gives you an edge over tough competitors

Enough flexibility to scale a business, increasing visibility and engagement

Showcase creative abilities without restrictions

Cons:

Setting up several business elements can be confusing if not organized properly.

In some cases, the start-up doesn't scale through as the individual has other ideas that override the initial business idea.

Start-Up Cost

Starting a business hinged on creativity comes with less cost. The unique selling point here is creativity. This element sets your start-up apart from others. Most creative, on-demand skills require that you have the following:

A PC

Internet connectivity

Software

Other relevant gadgets (printer, scanner, camera, et cetera)

If you already have these items available, then you are good to go. You may also need a website, business contact materials (flyers, brochure, and business card), and marketing.

How to Sell It/Suggested Businesses

When it comes to establishing a creative business, there is no perfect timing. You don't have to wait until it's all rainbow and sunshine. However, you still have to make preparations. Stalling until you have everything in place will only hinder you from taking advantage of opportunities. As your business kicks off, you can get other elements in place.

Besides, you don't have to rent office space to work as a graphic designer. You can achieve this from the comfort of your home. In fact, remote jobs and freelancing is the new are creating a revolution in the information age. So, how can you start a creative business?

Identify your passion. But is that all there is to it? Of course, no. You have to give your passion a purpose. This is the fuel needed to get your start-up off the ground.

What do you love to do the most? Is it in high demand? If yes, how can you monetize it? These are questions that will help you to make the right business decision.

Okay, you've nurtured that dream enough; it is time to convert it into reality? This is where planning comes into play. You have to create a plan to make your passion feasible. How do you want to launch your YouTube channel? Your startup should center around your mission.

For example, as a graphic designer, you should meet the following requirements:

Logo designing

Infographics

Poster designing

Brand strategy

Social media designing

Web designing

Brochure designing

Typography

Animation

Once your plan is in place, it is time to set up your start-up. You really started to describe the features and examined them one by one (no multi-tasking people).

You need the following in creating business outreach:

A logo

Website A website (valuable and detailed content about what you do)

One reason people come back (probably with a blog or newsletter)

Social media setup, strategy, and implementation.

There are huge loads of free instructional materials that you can discover on YouTube or Google. Canva provides the ideal platform to design custom logos using different available templates.

Users on the platform testify to it being user-friendly. Create the perfect business logo using the drag-and-drop elements. If you don't have the time or skill to get such a job done, you can outsource to a professional.

Create a buzz. It is time to inform the public about your services, so you shouldn't be cold about it. Business advertisement doesn't hinge on creating a couple of lines and posting them on Facebook – it doesn't work that way.

Have you noticed that large corporations, like Coca-Cola, spend millions of dollars on adverts and, as such, create the right response from their target audiences?

This is not to state that you should empty your life savings on your start-up advert. However, you should invest resources, like time, professionalism, effort, and many more, to ensure that you get engagement. You need to go all out as a start-up. Over time, your clients will do the talking, bringing more people to patronize your services.

Generate buzz the organic way, do the talking and let your skills back you up. You don't necessarily have to pay someone else to publicize your services, especially as a start-up. Such a move is not as powerful as going all out to showcase to visitors what you are up to. Let your social media accounts do the talking. Other interested individuals may share your services on their platforms.

It's about to get fast and furious. The launch date is closer than you expected. Like a ticking bomb, you are likely to go off all over the place. But you know what? Get yourself together. Fretting over the business launch date will do no good.

Take your time to map out a marketing schedule geared towards the special event. Ascertain where your potential clients are, regardless of whether it's on a specific web-based media platform or in an online group. At that point, get talking.

Connect with other individuals on the platform and share your launch program with them, indicating that you're energized and can't wait to share your services with them.

There are other business ideas you can launch as well. You could sell digital prints online, for example. It is worth noting that platforms like Etsy aren't only for craft sales; you can likewise sell digital documents for download. Professionals can exploit this by effectively utilizing their visual and creative skills and selling prints and outlines carefully.

You could offer various services, for example, divider banners that can be printed out, or offer variants of delightful cards for individuals to ship off their friends and family.

In the same vein, Instagram is likewise an incredible spot for selling your professional craftsmanship, utilizing Shopify, the web-based shopping platform.

A perfectly curated Instagram feed is an incredible show stopper, and the greater commitment and supporters you have, the more you're probably going to sell.

Sell your professional photos online. Several stock websites purchase stock photos from professional photographers. Most of these platforms have libraries fully packed with premium photos that are credited to their creators. You can also take advantage of such platforms to showcase your skills.

You may have an image library fully packed with mind-blowing pictures. It is time to show the world what you have. Your photos can range from wildlife to kitchen accessory photography.

If you have no idea about the stock photo site to use in showcasing your jobs, you may try Dreamstime, Shutterstock, and Getty Images. Some of these sites pay commission rates of up to 25%. Income may not be significant to live on, but it can meet those little needs.

Consider virtual tutoring. Content creation has exploded online, targeting children and adults alike. But you don't have to keep everything. Creativity has the desired skills that people want to learn at home, so why not create content for online education websites like Udemi or Skillshare?

People can take advantage of your courses to learn new things. A good smartphone camera to take pictures to teach yourself all you need.

Thousands of courses covering creative topics from photography to web design have already been uploaded, and you can join this mix. Make sure you are thinking of what unique insights you can offer. If you find this idea a little confusing, check out our public speaking tips.

You may have a knack for creating amazing fonts. Why not monetize such a skill? You can create your fonts and sell on platforms like YouWorkForThem or MyFonts. The former will partner with you to upgrade your fonts, complete font families, provide customer support, and many more.

YouWorkForThem also gives you a cut of products sold. On the other hand, you can sell your fonts directly on MyFonts. However, there are requirements for Font quality.

Estimated Earnings

Earning an income from your creative business depends on the type of skill you are providing. For example, copywriters earn an average pay of $38 per hour. These individuals write copy for marketing and advertising purposes.

Such materials may include emails, ad copy, articles, taglines, eBooks, and newsletters. They need to be well-versed in search engine optimization (SEO).

With a robust copywriting portfolio, you can create the right impression on the minds of your clients. Interestingly, you only need a PC, internet connection, and peripheral devices to launch this start-up.

Graphic designers earn an average pay of $36 per hour. Those individuals with more experience and skills can charge more for their services. Their roles include designing visual and aesthetics materials for advertising, packaging, and entertainment purposes, just to mention a few.

Such individuals are most likely to earn a degree in such related fields.

Programmers earn $38 per hour on average. They build

software applications using codes of respective programming languages. The codes translate the programmer's language (human language) into one that the computer understands and can execute (machine language). Programming languages include Java, C++, Python, PHP, Swift, and many more.

Software developers earn an hourly pay of $42 per hour. Their services are one of the most lucrative in the creative start-up industry. They design and develop software programs.

As a software developer, you have to code, debug, test, and troubleshoot scripts of codes. In the same vein, you should be well-versed in the following:

PHP

HTML

XML

Having a robust portfolio will give your software development business an edge over other competitors and increase earnings.

Web developers earn $35 per hour on average. They create websites using programming languages. Roles may include site maintenance. Web developers are no strangers to coding, which they can use to integrate media files to develop websites that meet user requirements.

Technical writers earn about $41 per hour. To earn such an income, or more, you should have vast experience in technical writing and certifications to back your skills. As a technical writer, your role entails clarifying complex and technical information. This profession encapsulates journals, instruction manuals, documents, and guides.

Conclusion

Creating and launching a start-up is no walk in the park. As discussed before, 90% of businesses in this category don't see the light of day due to several factors. However, with the right guide, you can create a successful start-up. As a recap, here are some steps to take:

Consider Your Motivation

Identify the factors that keep you motivated.

Motivation and commitment are very important when creating your own successful business. The following questions help you rate your level of motivation: Are you motivated enough? Are you fully committed?

If the answer is yes, you have scaled the toughest part of your business. Many people struggle to succeed in their business due to a lack of commitment and lack of energy and determination behind it. It may be tempting to throw in the towel when the start-up faces challenges. There may be times when you may struggle to secure projects.

But note that such periods and situations become your motivation to succeed and move forward. If you lack motivation, you may lose interest in your start-up business sooner than you think.

Identify a Solid Skillset

What are you good at? Even in a particular field, there are several sub-sections. For example, graphic design comprises different types:

Environmental graphic design

Publication graphic design

Packaging graphic design

Visual identity graphic design

Web design

Marketing & advertising graphic design

Illustration for graphic design

Motion graphic design

Each type comes with its skillset. So, you have to know what you are good at and monetize it. Understand what your target audience wants as well.

Versatility is Essential

Long gone are those days when one skill was enough to earn you a significant income. With the ever-increasing competition, you need additional experience, skill-sets, and certifications to stand out from your competitors.

You may be a graphic designer but have less knowledge of web design. Chances are that you may come across a client in need of both services. Someone else with both skills will secure the project. It is essential to acquire more knowledge. Learning never ends, except in the grave.

Identify your Market

Who makes up your target audience? Large corporate organizations? Or small-scale enterprises? Are you targeting a young audience? Perhaps, you have a fashion trend worth showcasing. With this, you can develop your marketing plan.

Map out Pricing

As you're well set to commence your own unique start-up, make it a duty to do some market research to identify the general rate. Collate detailed information on how top organizations in the industry set prices for different services.

Then, adopt the best pricing structure for your services. To attract clients, nurture them and improve business visibility, come down a little bit first. At this point, you need a plan to attract these individuals.

Try and offer the best deal. At the same time, ensure that you are not too cheap. Show your clients that you are providing them with the best deal and value. Always remember, most of these individuals are willing to pay the best for a premium service.

As a marketing strategy, divide your service quality into sections and give clients what they want to pay for.

Consider Legalities

When launching a start-up or taking a project, ensure that you discuss it with a lawyer. Learn about all the legal requirements related to setting up a start-up business, such as business registration and insurance.

Don't hesitate to discuss the following with your attorney – licensing, legal procedures, trademark, copyright, and tax requirements. You may need to work on refund policies, privacy, dispute handling, and other legal issues. It is worth noting that these factors depend on the size of your business.

Consider Other Experts in Your Field

Business growth does not rest solely on the entrepreneur's shoulders, especially when it starts expanding. There are other individuals and entities involved. You cant do everything on your own. In some cases, you need an extra hand.

You may find yourself handling cases or projects belonging to six or eight clients rather than one or two. Taking all these tasks at once will only lead to a breakdown, which will affect your health and that of the business.

Along the line, keep a receptive outlook about recruiting a few experts.

By doing so, you will have a professional team on standby to take on any project, regardless of its complexity. As such, your business services improve, increasing visibility and reputation. In truth, you need more hands on deck as you advance.

For example, you can add another service to your bookkeeping business; this can be financial planning. Not only do your clients have an organized financial process, but they also get advice on how to manage their finances. You could even become an asset manager.

Hiring the right team is not as easy as picking a set of random guys to play frisbee. You have to invest resources into getting these professionals. Consider it a long-term investment, which can be highly rewarding.

Select an Ideal Workspace

The workplace you have for your business relies upon your monetary capacity and customer base. On the off chance that you would prefer not to spend a lot on office space from the outset, you can launch your start-up from your home. Nonetheless, ensure your workstation is reasonable for conducting all businesses.

You should be protected from all side-attractions and interruptions. As your business develops, you might need to consider moving to a bigger office space to serve your clients better.

Having an ideal office is fundamental to guaranteeing demonstrable skills and incrementing profitability. Getting the best space will establish a decent connection with your customers or clients.

Procure the Right Equipment or Gadget

You'll require a high-performance PC, proficient applications, and efficient gadgets or tools to offer your clients the best support.

Even though some of the startups require you communicating with the client physically, you will also communicate with them virtually via phone calls, websites, emails, video calls, and many more. You need the right gadget to make it happen.

If your services involve working manually, then you need the right equipment or tools to undertake clients' projects. For creative startups like graphic design, web design, mobile development, and content creation, it is essential to have efficient software that can perform such tasks.

Your significant input towards building a sophisticated business framework can guarantee your client-base expert support. So, it is time to turn your ideas into a profitable business, offering you and your clients a win-win outcome.